SYSTEMS

to Transform Your

Classroom and School

NANCIE ATWELL

SYSTEMS
to Transform Your
Classroom and School

HEINEMANN
Portsmouth, NH

Heinemann
361 Hanover Street
Portsmouth, NH 03801–3912
www.heinemann.com

Offices and agents throughout the world

The author and publisher wish to thank those who have generously given permission to reprint borrowed material in this book and/or on the DVD:

Cover image from *Stealing Buddha's Dinner: A Memoir* by Bich Minh Nguyen. Copyright © 2008 by Bich Minh Nguyen. Used by permission of Viking Penguin, a division of Penguin Young Readers Group, a member of Penguin Group (USA) Inc., New York.

Cover image and interior pages from *The Ghosts of Ashbury High* by Jaclyn Moriarty. Copyright © 2010 by Jaclyn Moriarty. Used by permission of Scholastic Inc., New York.

Excerpt from "Keep a Poem in Your Pocket" from *Something Special* by Beatrice Schenk de Regniers. Copyright ©1958, 1986 by Beatrice Schenk de Regniers. Used by permission of Marian Reiner.

Cover image from *Free-Range Chickens* by Simon Rich. Copyright © 2008 by Simon Rich. Used by permission of Random House, Inc., New York. Any third-party use of this material, outside of this publication, is prohibited. Interested parties must apply directly to Random House, Inc. for permission.

"When I lost my first tooth" from *Free-Range Chickens* by Simon Rich. Copyright © 2008 by Simon Rich. Used by permission of Levine Greenberg Literary Agency, Inc., New York.

Cataloging-in-Publication Data is on file at the Library of Congress.
ISBN-13: 978-0-325-04266-4

All royalties from the sale of this product support tuition assistance at the Center for Teaching and Learning, a non-profit demonstration school in Edgecomb, Maine.

Acquisitions Editor: Margaret LaRaia
Production Editor: Patricia Adams
Videographer: Kevin Carlson
DVD Production: Sherry Day and Stacy Holly
Cover and Interior Designs: Suzanne Heiser and Monica Ann Crigler
Typesetter: Gina Poirier Design
Manufacturing: Steve Bernier

Printed in the United States of America on acid-free paper
17 16 15 14 13 VP 1 2 3 4 5

Contents

Introduction

The Center for Teaching and Learning (CTL) is a K–8 demonstration school founded and run by teachers. This means huge, sometimes daunting responsibilities. But it also means the freedom to ask—and answer—the big questions: What matters in teaching writing, reading, math, history, science, and the arts? Which are the most effective methods in terms of what we know about child development, educational research, and learning theory? How do we help every child become engaged and skilled? What measures of assessment will both identify students' challenges and encourage their growth? Most important of all, who do we want our students to be when they leave here? While for us these are school-wide questions, posed in collaboration, they are the same questions every good teacher anywhere asks and strives to answer.

Because CTL is a demonstration school, one of our missions is to experiment for the good of children. The DVD depicts the practices developed by a cadre of like-minded teacher-researchers. The systems in place in our classes and the school as a whole illustrate how we act on our observations, beliefs, and experience to help students develop voices, choices, habits of mind, knowledge, skills, and a sense of belonging to something that's bigger than they are.

That something is a community, one where every child feels noticed and *known*. We've learned that whether it's one classroom or a whole building, there are steps teachers and administrators can take that make a class or school a place that's safe for children, one where students feel engaged and motivated, one that challenges kids and entices them with the intrinsic rewards of real work done well. We invite teachers to consider our systems and borrow from them—to enlarge your practice by adopting and adapting ours.

You'll learn about our workshops—the approach we use in K–8 to teach writing, reading, and mathematics. The workshop, a legacy of writer and researcher Donald Graves, is an invitation to apprenticeship and independence. It balances instruction to the whole group with individual initiative and activity, and it provides a reliable, predictable structure for teaching and learning at every grade level. CTL teachers appreciate the workshop model for its rigor, versatility, and responsiveness to children.

The workshop begins with students gathered in a circle for a warm-up or minilesson. Then children engage in independent or small-group work as writers, readers, or mathematicians, while the teacher circulates among them, provides guidance and assistance, and introduces new skills, strategies, and ideas in context.

Through a workshop apprenticeship, children learn how to identify their intentions, work on problems and toward goals, build on their strengths, and perceive the teacher's advice as practical and trustworthy. Teachers get to be maximally effective, first by creating a rich framework for the whole group via the minilesson and then, in conversations with individuals and small groups, inviting students to think aloud, ask questions, apply lessons, learn from their teacher and peers, and move forward.

This book introduces other methods developed by CTL teachers to meet our students' needs. Innovations are a hallmark of a professional teacher—of someone who observes and responds to what children can't yet do but might, with the right invitation. You'll see how Helene Coffin engages kindergartners in shared reading sessions: instead of one student approaching the chart to fill in a missing word while the others watch and wait, she gives all the children little spiral notebooks in which they record their guesses of the words she omitted from the class message. You'll see Jill Cotta, CTL's teacher of grades 3–4, write badly on purpose as a way to invite students to tease out and name what a good writer does. Ted DeMille and his first and second graders share some of the smart uses to which they put individual whiteboards. Glenn Powers and his fifth and sixth graders introduce the reader's roundtable and the rich possibilities for literary discussion even when every student is reading a different book, while the middle-school students of Katie Rittershaus research and present about great mathematical thinkers in order to understand how mathematicians collaborate, experiment, stumble, and outright fail on the way to their breakthroughs.

All of this activity occurs in the context of a deliberate culture created and sustained by teachers. This is where I'll start—with the rituals and traditions that define our school community, from shared poems and songs, inside and outside shoes, and a kazoo band, to continuous conversations, daily morning meetings, a school bill of rights that children and teachers composed and revisit every five years, and the adoption, K–8, of Vivian Paley's essential social rule, "You can't say you can't play," which for over twenty years has defined inclusiveness at our school and denied a foothold to meanness and bullying.

Finally, a word about our students. They are regular kids. Because CTL teachers disseminate our methods, because other teachers come to the school to observe us in action, we handpick a

Front view of CTL, a pre-fab Cape: two wings were added as we added grades.

Rear View of School Building

student body that represents a diversity of socioeconomic backgrounds and ability levels. CTL parents work hard, as farmers, carpenters, house cleaners and house painters, soldiers, retail workers, fishermen and lobstermen, landscapers, musicians, nurses, physicians, teachers, and small business owners. We keep tuition as low as possible—at a rate that's one third that of comparable local independent schools—and we offer generous assistance. Almost 80% of students receive some form of reduction in tuition.

CTL is not an elite private school. It's the nonprofit of all time, a labor of love and professional commitment and an institution that, since 1990, has done what charter schools said they were going to do: we seek to innovate, and then we pass along the lessons learned to our public-school colleagues everywhere.

"Classroom teachers take responsibility to pay attention to our students' social lives and to talk with them about issues we observe or that kids bring to us."

1

School Traditions

Talk About It and Reflect

- A tradition is the enactment of a belief. What are some of the traditions and customs of your classroom and school?
- What beliefs—about children, learning, parents, teaching, and community—inform your classroom and school traditions? How does each one benefit children by having a direct impact on their social and academic lives?
- Could your students identify the core of beliefs at the heart of your classroom? Your school?

Read About CTL Traditions

The overarching goal of tradition in a classroom or school is to give students an opportunity to say, "This is the way we do things here. This is how we treat one another. These are the beliefs and customs that bind us, and I'm a part of it all." CTL's social traditions carry over into academics because they give every student a sense of belonging to a community.

Our essential tradition is the social rule established by Vivian Paley: "You can't say you can't play." CTL teachers forbid exclusion. Children have to figure out—often with help from faculty and peers—how to allow other children to join their play. We mandate it: "Everyone is a member of this community, everyone is valued, and everyone gets included."

We instituted Paley's rule early on in the school's history. When we heard one child saying to another, "I don't want to play with you," or "She's my best friend, and besides, only two can play this game," we recognized that the worst things that happen to kids at school are social—a peer insults or excludes them. Paley refers to this as the young child's "habit of rejection," and it's apparent right from the first day of kindergarten. If unaddressed, it institutionalizes meanness. We teachers wrestled with questions: How can kids learn to include everyone? How might acceptance and teamwork become school customs?

After CTL opened its door in 1990 as a K–3 school, the teachers spent a lot of time orchestrating role-plays at our daily, all-school morning meetings. Small groups of kids enacted problematic situations that had arisen, often on the playground, and the others analyzed what had gone wrong and suggested solutions. Teachers coached the role-players beforehand and mediated the discussion that followed. In addition, whenever we got wind of an incidence of meanness, individual teachers stopped class to moderate a discussion with our students. We intervened until a healthy consensus was reached. Although many principles of life at CTL are democratic and choice-based, inclusion isn't one of them. Acceptance is the rule.

Because we devote consistent, significant time to communal problem-solving, the cult of best friend-ism, a prime excuse for excluding others, doesn't exist at CTL. But we're no utopia. Problems will always arise, and kids will continue to role-play and discuss hurtful social situations at morning meeting. Just this week four eighth-grade boys reenacted how an unnamed kindergartner had been changing his seat at lunch whenever the "wrong" peers joined his table, while a group of fifth graders showed what happened when a game of tag turned into an angry confrontation. It makes a difference in a child's day when he knows he can walk fearlessly into a classroom or onto the playground and, if he should ever need it, there's a mechanism in place to shine a light on acts of rejection and meanness and put a stop to them.

"You can't say you can't play" inspired other social rules. Teachers established a policy that students and their parents can't deliver party invitations at school unless everyone in the class is invited. We teach older students to preserve myths—Santa Claus, the Tooth Fairy, the Easter

The 7–8 Group at Lunch, with Science Teacher Sally Macleod

Bunny, and St. Patrick's Day leprechauns—for the younger children, to celebrate their own burgeoning maturity while cherishing the little ones and their beliefs.

Our students eat lunch with their teachers in classrooms, and every day at noon, the kids in grades 5–8 push together all the desks or tables in their classrooms to form a big table around which everyone sits and is a member of the luncheon party. It's a pain in the neck to move all that furniture twice a day, but it's worth it. Everyone's included; no one sits alone.

Classroom teachers take responsibility to pay attention to our students' social lives and to talk with them about issues we observe or that kids bring to us. Jill Cotta, grades 3–4 teacher, schedules regular luncheons with just the boys or just the girls in her class, to keep on top of social dynamics and help her students process peer problems.

When an act of misbehavior or meanness occurs among my middle-grade students, I gather the offenders at lunchtime in another room and ask them to write, read, and talk about what happened. For example, after Nikki confided that she felt ostracized by the other eighth- grade girls, I wrote at the top of a piece of paper "Nikki has been feeling isolated and criticized. What

> Nikki has been feeling isolated and criticized among the 8th grade girls. What are your observations? What role have you played?
>
> I've noticed recently that this has been happening. [crossed out] on Friday a couple of my friends a/ invited her to help us plan the drama?
>
> This happens often. I stay with my brother at snack so I don't have to deal with being ignored. During recess, I try to make excuses like helping people in math, so I won't have to be alone outside. Just being invited to come outside would be something new, or knowing someone in my grade actually would like to spend time with me.
>
> If you come outside we would love for you to join us, but we didn't know these were excuses. We thought you actually wanted to help in math.
>
> Hearing rumors about Nikki — she has no friends, she makes all these excuses to be alone — made me actually believe that she hated us. I thought Nikki was isolating herself on purpose, but one could assume that she was afraid of rejection and that isolation could save her from that. I just think we've been blind to the obvious details.
>
> I also thought that Nikki didn't want to hang out with us the way she sat with teachers at lunch, I thought she didn't want to be around me or the other girls I don't know how I missed the tell-tale signs, but I did and I feel terrible about that. I thought Nikki liked teaching people math stuff at recess.

Figure 1.1 Written Conversation Among "Nikki" and Her Peers

role have you played?" I made photocopies, gathered the eighth-grade girls around a table, gave a paper headed with the question to each one, and asked them to write in response—no talking. After a few minutes, I asked each to pass her paper to the girl on her right, read the previous writer's comment, and write beneath it. When everyone had written on and read every page, I skimmed them and asked the girls, "Do you want me to stay and lead a conversation? Or would you like to process this by yourselves?" What they had written showed me that this was less a case of meanness than misunderstanding. When they said they wanted to handle it themselves, I left them to it, and the misunderstandings and Nikki's hurt feelings ended there. She was relieved, and her friends swallowed a strong dose of empathy. Figure 1.1 shows one of the pages of their written conversation.

Rituals like these represent explicit strategies for governing student behavior and establishing a healthy community. Others set a tone. I'm thinking of such traditions as our school symbols, oak trees and acorns, which were inspired by the giant red oak at the edge of our playground; our school poem, Mary Oliver's "The Summer Day"; and the round we sing together on the first and last days of school, "This Pretty Planet" by Tom Chapin. Every student knows our song and poem by heart—a phrase that implies both the significance of the lyrics and how we raise our voices in common purpose.

Other traditions and rituals emerge when something cool happens and the teachers recognize and want to hold onto it. The school's acreage includes an imaginary village called

Eighth Graders Wallace and Xander in Country Town with Their Second-Grade Fort

"Country Town," established twenty years ago by children who looked at the woods behind the building and saw forts. I challenge an adult to trek beyond the stone wall and see anything but

A Game of Six-Square-and-an-Apartment at Recess

big piles of sticks, but there is a village, and it has evolved for two decades because teachers provide opportunities for children to talk about Country Town at morning meeting, write poems and memoirs about it, and invent and reinvent their imaginary community.

Another playground ritual was adapted by my students years ago from the traditional schoolyard

Morning Ping-Pong

game of four square. Ours is called six square and an apartment, and by now it involves more than a hundred "taps," most of them elaborate and ridiculous. In September, a joyful part of a seventh grader's initiation into the 7–8 group is learning the taps and taking his or her place in a square—or the apartment.

Our fifth- and sixth-grade boys and girls play their own version of touch football at rainless recesses in the fall and spring. Before morning meeting, early arrivals play Ping-Pong on classroom desks they push together. The teachers supply playground chalk, balls, paddles, and applause. We've learned to notice and encourage opportunities for kids to be playful—and active—together.

Running jokes that everyone can laugh at, because everyone gets them, are another tradition we cultivate. When flocks of wild turkeys began to haunt our part of Maine, we adapted the lyrics of some of the morning-meeting songs to reflect the kids' obsession with turkeys and started a collection of turkey art. We also have fun with a favorite song of our kindergarten teacher Helene Coffin, "When the Red, Red Robin Comes Bob, Bob, Bobbin' Along." On her birthday each April, she appears at morning meeting dressed as a giant, red-breasted bird and dances in front of a chorus line of her former students, as the rest of us sing to her. And Glenn Powers, teacher of grades 5–6, is famous for his display of disgust at the sight of a wiggly tooth. You can bet he gets to see lots of them.

A practical school tradition is the way teachers signal for silence: right hand on left shoulder. We determined that adults will not raise their voices at our school because we want to demonstrate good manners and respect. The simple gesture of a hand on a shoulder, accompanied by an attitude of watchful expectation, teaches students to notice when an adult needs quiet, and they (eventually) comply.

The school estimation jar is an academic tradition. Every month, on a rotating schedule, one of the teachers fills it with a number of something: marbles, cotton balls, Matchbox cars, acorns, Swedish fish, paper clips, candy conversation hearts, even grains of rice. Then the teacher places a known quantity of the same item in an extrapolation jar of a comparable size, notes on its lid how many it contains, and gives kids a week or two to submit estimates. We announce the top five or six guesses at morning meeting, and the student who came closest describes his or her process. The idea for the estimation jar was born at a lunchtime faculty meeting where we brainstormed about how to initiate more communal math, to parallel the

The Estimation and Extrapolation Jars

way the whole school reads a poem and the lyrics of a song every morning. We also instituted occasional whole-school "wordy problem" competitions: multistep word problems that involve a seasonal topic or one the student body is studying in history or science (Figure 1.2).

Other traditions that emerge at CTL relate to the calendar. In January, I'll announce, at a morning meeting, "It's grey, and it's going to be grey. We need to lift our spirits: let's schedule a Beach Day." We talk about appropriate garb, and kids and teachers come to school dressed for

---

Start with the square root of 9.

Add the date in December on which Hanukkah begins this year.

Subtract the number of candles on a menorah, *including* the shamash.

Square that number.

Subtract the date in December on which Boxing Day falls.

Your answer will equal the exact number of snowballs kids will throw at CTL this winter.

Show your work. Be sure to put your name on your entry.

Figure 1.2 December Wordy Problem

hot summer weather and a limbo dance competition. We celebrate Orange and Black Day on October 31; Pajama Day on the first day back from winter break, when we open an hour late; Stuffie Day, when we meet children's old favorite stuffed toys; Cinco de Mayo with piñatas, games, and a feast; Chinese New Year with a dragon dance and a feast; a Passover seder; Easter egg dyeing and hunts; in March, the creation of leprechaun houses and artifacts by the big kids for the little ones to find; and Earth Day in April with a K–8 playground cleanup and the planting of pansy seedlings. When the faculty considered the various winter holidays of different religions and cultures, we decided we could either ignore them all or embrace them all. So we honor everything—the solstice, Christmas, Hanukkah, Kwanzaa, even Boxing Day. Our kids enjoy opportunities to learn about many traditions and to teach the stories and symbols of their own religions and cultures.

Practical traditions abound. We ask every K–6 student to keep and wear a pair of "inside shoes" or slippers at school: no boots or outside shoes are allowed because the carpeted floors are used as work spaces. This custom has countless ramifications for how children feel comfortable

A Passover Seder at Recess

at their school throughout the day—when they gather in a circle on the floor for minilessons, read lying down, or collaborate on small-group projects.

The tradition of school jobs began when tired teachers asked, "How do we help kids take responsibility for the building? How do we make this their place, too?" Today, every student in grades 1–8 is assigned, by his or her teacher, to a particular job for a month at a time. Children pour milk, sharpen pencils, check supplies in classrooms, recycle and compost, put chairs up or take them down, pour milk, wipe down tables after lunch, vacuum after snack, and ring the school bell to end recess, while the job of every kindergartner all year long is to learn how to "do school," including taking responsibility for their belongings and the school's resources. Jobs are another way for students to say, "This is my school, and this is how I help take care of it, in addition to learning how to organize and take care of my own things."

Student Cubbies with Overnight Bookbags and Inside Shoes

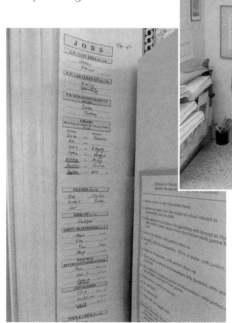

Mac performs her job, ringing the recess bell.

These are family-like responsibilities, customs, jokes, and activities. They help teachers assume parent-like roles in students' lives: we're all on the same team. This camaraderie is another reason

The Monthly Jobs Posting

we experience fewer behavior problems at CTL than anywhere any of us previously taught. Rituals reinforce community. This is a gentle environment, but it's also one that rings with debate and laughter. There's minimal meanness, much mutual respect, and constant conversation. The last is the most important tradition of all.

Teachers expect our students to raise their hands to speak, so that one child at a time has the floor. At every grade level we teach how to listen and respond with respect, and we call kids on it when they don't. When teacher-interns visit CTL, they comment on how considerate our students' discussions are. We're gratified to hear it but quick to respond that this isn't an accident—this is school policy.

Every teacher *listens* to children. Each of us invites conversations and debates that are based on evidence and informed by relevant vocabulary. While writing-across-the-curriculum plays a huge role in promoting thoughtfulness and knowledge acquisition, teachers foster and referee sustained talk of depth and breadth in every subject, all day long.

Conversations solve small problems before they become big ones, air issues, settle arguments, set agendas, determine criteria, generate ideas, articulate discoveries, create empathy, analyze experience, tap the lexicons of the arts and sciences, and spark action, progress, and laughter. If I had to start all over again tomorrow, my first and foremost expectation would be that children and teachers spend significant amounts of time talking and listening to one another.

Moving-Up Ceremony on the Last Day of School

Develop Your Own Traditions

Traditions are a way to honor beliefs through actions. Some examples from our school, as shown in the chart, might provide inspiration for yours.

Because we believe that . . .	we:
students will grow as individuals and learners,	• plant pumpkin seedlings with the incoming kindergartners each May, so they can harvest them in October. • after kindergarten, assign students to double-grade groups (1–2, 3–4, 5–6, and 7–8), so they benefit from the insights of teachers and peers who know them as individuals and learners. • in late May, schedule a "step-up" morning that K–7 children spend with next year's teacher and classmates, while the eighth graders breakfast off-site.
students and teachers are members of a community,	• hold a daily morning meeting: a ritual of announcements, celebrations, problem-solving, songs, and poetry. • during the first week of school, schedule a field day at a local campground where teachers gather our new groups and help them bond via games and team activities. • collaborate on a school-wide bill of rights, which we revisit every five years. • assign fourth graders as reading buddies to kindergartners and instruct them about how to tutor beginning readers. • create our own holidays, like Stuffie Day and Pajama Day. • teach a five-year spiral curriculum in science and history, in which all students, K–8, study the same topics and concepts, while their teachers plan cross-grade activities.

(Continues)

Because we believe that . . .	we:
we should care and know about one another,	• sing to children on their birthdays at morning meeting, celebrate all the summer birthdays on the last day of school, and enjoy such silliness as asking each birthday boy or girl, "Did you have breakfast in bed?" • schedule an annual collections fair, where children and teachers display items from their personal collections, from rocks, geodes, and shells to toy hedgehogs, bottle caps, Matchbox cars, rubber duckies, and refrigerator magnets. • accept for publication every piece of writing submitted to *Acorns*, our nonjuried K–8 literary magazine. • celebrate every child's promotion to the next grade at a moving-up ceremony in June, with a handshake, certificate of moving up, and wild applause for each of them.
parents deserve and need to partner with their children's teachers and be kept in the loop,	• call all of our students' parents in early September, plus the kindergarten teacher makes home visits in August. • send home a newsletter every Friday about students' activities. • publish teachers' phone numbers, e-mail addresses, and the best times to reach us. • write, revise, and distribute a detailed yet friendly parent handbook. • ask parents to call teachers by our first names. • orchestrate a graduation ceremony in June at which all the eighth graders speak—to parents, relatives, and friends—about who they have become at CTL.

Complete a chart like this one, based on the beliefs that inform your school or classroom and the traditions you might create and celebrate. As the school year progresses, look for customs to add to the list. Recognize that the traditions at CTL were developed over years, and focus on a few meaningful additions at a time.

Tap Resources About Traditions

In terms of resources that help teachers help kids learn how to be good to one another, we recommend that every K–8 school's professional library contain copies of *You Can't Say You Can't Play* by Vivian Gussin Paley (Harvard University Press). CTL teachers also appreciate *Choice Words* by Peter Johnston (Stenhouse) and *Sticks and Stones: Defeating the Culture of Bullying and Rediscovering the Power of Character and Empathy* by Emily Bazelon (Random House), and *Schools Where Everyone Belongs: Practical Strategies for Reducing Bullying* by Stan Davis (Research Press).

The *Systems* DVD includes three documents by CTL faculty that you may find useful to adapt or adopt:

- Student Job Chart
- Communication with Parents
- Sample Weekly Newsletter

Communication with Parents

The Newsletter

Our primary means of school-to-home communication is a weekly newsletter, printed on blue paper so parents can learn to look for it by color. We send a copy home to each CTL household every Friday afternoon. In the lead section, the head of school provides information about upcoming field trips and special programs, presents opportunities for parent volunteers, explains or reviews school policies and procedures, highlights the accomplishments of individual students, and acknowledges contributions from parents and kids.

The newsletter continues with a weekly report by each classroom teacher about the activities and accomplishments of our groups, by subject area. These "Highlights of the Week" are intended as a source of information for parents, as well as a conversation-starter at home about a child's academic pursuits and activities. The newsletter concludes with a calendar of upcoming school events and a poem written by a student.

Each teacher's weekly highlights paragraph follows a similar format:

- Describe highligh…
  (e.g., writing wo…
- Use a we voice, …
- Avoid jargon: pa…
- Submit double-…
  by Thursday aft…

The Parent Ha…

I revise the CTL Par…
tents. It outlines sch…
from when and whe…
tips on how to read …
Question," which pr…
arise that aren't add…
another parent, whe…
they address us by o…
them as the adults w…

Homework an…

In a first-week-of-sch…
discuss and decide w…
assure parents that w…
thing we ask student…
able to participate in …

We provide every…
is for the benefit of p…
in the evening and c…

© 2014 by Nancie A…

Student Job Chart

JOBS

A.M. Cubbie Area Clean-Up (Gr. 1–6)

-
-

P.M. Lab Clean-Up (Gr. 7–8)

-
-

P.M. Humanities Clean-Up (Gr. 5–6)

-
-

Chairs

Morning		Afternoon	
•		(M/S) •	(M/S)
•		(M/S) •	(M/S)
•		(W) •	(W)
•		(W) •	(W)
•		(H) •	(H)
•		(H) •	(H)
•		(L) •	(L)
•		(L) •	(L)

Sample Weekly Newsletter to Parents

March 1

Dear Parents,

Glenn's class was featured in last Saturday's *Portland Press Herald*. "Classroom in the Pines" illustrated their yearlong study as citizen scientists at the Hidden Valley Nature Center. We've attached a copy of the article; links to the video and slideshow are available at http://www.pressherald.com/sports/thats-learning-by-nature_2013-02-24.html. Kudos to Glenn and the fifth- and sixth-grade environmental scientists. On Wednesday, Cynthia gave a wonderful presentation on the Baha'i Festival of Ayyam-i-Ha, which is celebrated between February 25 and March 1. Thanks, Cynthia.

The second trimester ends next week, and soon after portfolio conferences commence. Spring can't be too far off.

Please Complete the Attached Surveys

Attached you'll find five surveys designed by seventh- and eighth-grade students who are conducting original research as part of their work as essayists. They're counting on CTL parental assistance. Would you please complete the surveys that are appropriate to you and send them back to school on Monday, with instructions to give the surveys to Nancie at morning meeting? Thanks in advance for your cooperation. We'll include the resulting essays in future newsletters.

DaPonte String Quartet Returns to CTL

We are looking forward to next Friday morning's performance by the DaPonte String Quartet. Parents and family members are welcome to attend. The performance will be held in the Barn at 10:45. DaPonte cellist Myles Jordan, father of Noah and Max (CTL '11), has again offered us an opportunity to appreciate the quartet's work, and we are most grateful.

Mathcounts Team Heads to Regional Competition on Saturday

Best of luck to our talented mathletes—Xander, Wallace, Amelia, Claire D-R, Teagan, Payton, Sophia S., Nicholas, Charlotte, Emily, and Tristam—who will represent CTL at the regional Mathcounts competition on Saturday at Kennebec Valley Community College in Fairfield. The team, under the guidance of Katie and coach Alex D-R, has been preparing on Thursday afternoons since fall. The college is located adjacent to exit 132 on I-95 northbound, twenty-one miles north of Augusta. *Please make sure your son or daughter packs a lunch and drinks and arrives rested, with a full night's sleep.* It is also essential that students bring their TI-83+ calculators and extra batteries.

March Madness Swimming Starts Soon: Volunteers Needed

The tradition continues. On March 18, we will begin four weeks of Monday afternoon swimming lessons for students in grades K–2 at the Wiscasset Community Center. The program replaces Pam's regular phys ed program during that time and is a great bridge between the depths of winter and warm spring weather, when we can return to the great outdoors.

If you can help drive or chaperone on any one of the four Mondays, please indicate your willingness on the permission form; don't forget to sign up on the Writing Room calendar, too. We're particularly in need of a few dads to help staff the boys' locker room.

"Morning meeting is a jumping-off point for the day. Instead of homeroom or 'hang up your coat, and then it's time for math,' we segue into school life with a chance to check in, rub shoulders with one another, and engage as members of a community."

2

Morning Meeting

Talk About It and Reflect

Before you learn about a typical morning meeting at CTL, consider the following questions.

- How does a day begin at your school? Select a student, and describe what he or she experiences upon arrival in the morning. What feels positive and predictable? What helps a child achieve a sense of security and belonging? What do you wish happened otherwise?

- Now think about the beginning of your day as a teacher or administrator. What are your first interactions with students as they enter your classroom or school? With colleagues? What feels positive and predictable? What helps you achieve a sense of security and belonging? What do you wish happened otherwise?

- What are positive characteristics of your school— traditions, symbols, and special events? How are these acknowledged and enjoyed by the whole community? Which ones *don't* involve athletics?

- How and when do teachers collaborate to define, demonstrate, and expect the values and behaviors you want students to adopt school-wide?

Read About Morning Meeting

We start every day at CTL with a whole-school meeting: fifteen or twenty minutes devoted to announcements, current events, relevant topics in science and history, birthday celebrations, a poem, and a song. It's the most purposeful and joyful way I know to begin a school day. The choral effect of raised voices invigorates us and puts everyone on the same page. We exit morning meeting with the same song on our lips and poem on our minds. And we learn all kinds of things about one another.

Morning meeting is a jumping-off point for the day. Instead of homeroom or "hang up your coat, and then it's time for math," we segue into school life with a chance to check in, rub shoulders with one another, and engage as members of a community. I know many teachers who orchestrate morning meetings in their classrooms or within the wing of a school building. Whatever the format, this gathering should feel like a smart, loving family starting its day together. Many of the beliefs and traditions that undergird our school emerged from something that happened at a morning meeting.

With everyone on a pillow on the floor, with little kids on big kids' laps, with voices raised as one, and with every member's birthday acknowledged, we create our community. To celebrate his or her birthday, each child or teacher gets a personalized birthday sticker and chooses from among three songs: "Happy Birthday," "It Makes Me Think of the Good Old Days," or the Beatles'

A Dragon Dance to Celebrate the Chinese New Year

"Birthday." In September, the seventh and eighth graders learn how to play the Beatles' bass line on the kazoo, and their band gets into the act if that's the song of choice. We always pitch in afterwards with "Feliz Cumpleaños."

Morning meeting is an opportunity for kids who have lost teeth to show the new gaps; it's a chance to describe animal sightings or circulate a cool photograph, a foreign coin, or a natural find, like a bird's

The Birthday-Sticker Folder

nest or a horseshoe crab. It's show-and-tell, except the teachers determined that certain topics don't work here. A l-o-n-g story, an announcement about a new toy, or a discussion of an upsetting current event don't have a place at a gathering of a K–8 community.

Morning meeting is the time to solve school problems. If noon recess sledding has become dangerous, we collaborate to review the rules for the sledding hill. If teachers need to think something through together—the song selections for the winter holiday program or how to group classes for a field trip—we often use morning meeting as the occasion for our discussion. Kids hear their teachers solving a dilemma or addressing an issue.

Children don't hear enough constructive adult talk, enough of the voices of grown-ups putting their shoulders to a common wheel. They need to be able to eavesdrop on the conversations that make the wheel turn. This benefits them in peer relationships as they try to solve their own problems, but also later on. As teachers, we aim to be the kind of adults children would like to grow up to become. A part of that is their listening to well-meaning adults figure things out together. Of all the modeling our faculty does, consciously or not, our morning-meeting exchanges are an essential demonstration of what productive conversation sounds like.

Morning meeting also serves a structural purpose. Any child's school day is filled with transitions. We try to be thoughtful about students' transitions and make them easy to navigate. A break between arriving at

We celebrate Jack's seventh birthday.

Ted's Group in the Reading Room at 8:50

Glenn's Group in the Reading Room at 10:40 in a Reader's Roundtable

Jill's Group in the Reading Room at 1:05

school and beginning the academic day helps individuals settle themselves and also gather as members of a group. Children tend to sit with students from their classes, but there's a lot of lap-sitting, too. At the end of morning meeting, the teacher who's in the chair that week dismisses students by class to the content-area rooms where they'll launch into their academic day: "The mathematicians in Glenn's group, please head to the Lab…. Jill's writers, gather in the Writing Room…. Helene's writers and readers, you're dismissed to the Play Place for your poem of the day…. Nancie, Katie, and Sally's group, move on over to the Humanities Room for writing-reading workshop." Even dismissal is deliberate at CTL.

The content-area rooms I just referenced are shared teaching spaces. All the classrooms at CTL are shared. In 1990, when the school opened in a pre-fab Cape, we had two classes—a K–1 and a 2–3—and no money. So we pooled resources and equipped one classroom for math and science and the other for writing and reading. Halfway through the day, the teachers and their classes swapped rooms.

As we added grades and built additions to the school, we kept the model. It continues to save money as students share computers, math manipulatives, science equipment, books, and other resources. But content-area rooms also invite students to take on the affect of the discipline to which a room is dedicated:

I'll think and act as a reader here…now, I'm a scientist. In addition, there's none of the pent-up energy of children who sit at one desk in one room all day long.

Transitions among the content-area rooms occur at natural breaks in the school day. After everyone begins together with

Storage Bins of Poems and Songs on Charts

morning meeting at 8:30, each group and its teacher go off to work in one of the content-area classrooms until a snack recess at 10:15. At 10:30, they gather in another content-area room until lunch. After noon recess, they settle in a third room until dismissal. There are no bells. It is a reliable, predictable schedule. Content-area rooms are a great model for single-grade teams of teachers within a big school, as well as a small rural school like ours, or a school-within-a-school. Figure 2.1 shows CTL's basic, no specials, block schedule.

Another essential morning-meeting lesson involves everyone reading the words of a poem and the lyrics to a song. Teachers have printed more than four hundred songs and four hundred poems—some written by professionals, some by kids, and some by us—on oak tag charts. There are many ways for people to learn how to work together. Work that doesn't feel like drudgery, that promises a sense of gratification, is the most worthwhile. Singing is work we do together. We make a joyful noise—our kids sound great. And singing helps them develop public voices. For most students, it becomes natural—just another of the things they do at their school.

It helps that Ted DeMille is a professional musician and an outstanding guitar player. But before Ted joined the faculty, we owned a CD player and a decent collection of disks to sing along to. These days, in addition to Ted, the school has an iPod that's loaded with tunes we have charts for. I've included on the *Systems* DVD a sampling of the songs and poems we've charted for morning meeting.

We want our students to grow up to be good citizens—to attend town meetings and speak up, to have opinions and voice them. Any time or way we can invite children to raise their voices—whether it's announcing to the school that they've lost a tooth and showing the gap, describing how great-grandma's frugal habits illustrate what it means to be a "Depression baby," collaborating on a list of things to do during a rainy-day recess, reporting how the Mathcounts team fared at the state meet, telling about the first robin sighting, or singing—it prepares them for the constructive public roles we hope they'll take on as adults.

Center for Teaching and Learning Basic Schedule					
	Helene (K)	Ted (1–2)	Jill (3–4)	Glenn (5–6)	Nancie, Sally, & Katie (7–8)
8:30–8:45	MORNING MEETING IN READING ROOM: CURRENT EVENTS, ANNOUNCEMENTS, BIRTHDAYS, A SONG, A POEM				
8:45–10:15	Circle Time & Poetry Time 8:45–9:30 (Play Place) Math/Science 9:30–10:15 (Math/Science Room)	Reading (Reading Room)	Writing/ Spelling (Writing Room)	Math/ Science (The Lab)	Writing/ Spelling/ Reading (Humanities Room)
10:15–10:35	SNACK RECESS ON THE FIRST FLOOR				
10:35–12:05	Reading 10:35–11:15 (Primary Reading Room) Writing 11:15–12:05 (Play Place)	Writing/ Spelling/ History (Writing Room)	Math/ Science (Math/ Science Room)	Reading/ History (Reading Room)	History 10:35–11:20 (Humanities Room) Science or Math 11:20–12:05 (The Lab)
12:05–1:00	LUNCH FOR ALL IN THE LAB/PLAY PLACE/MATH-SCIENCE ROOM/HUMANITIES ROOM; RECESS AT 12:25				
1:00–2:45	Rest and Story 1:00–1:30 (Play Place) Activity Time 1:30–2:15 Free Time 2:15–2:45	Math/ Science (Math/ Science Room)	Reading/ History (Reading Room)	Writing/ Spelling (Humanities Room)	Math or Science (The Lab)

Figure 2.1 Center for Teaching and Learning Basic Schedule

Watch a Morning Meeting

As you watch a typical morning meeting at CTL, notice the format. It's predictable. We start with student and teacher announcements, and then move on to birthday celebrations, academic or social business, a poem, and a song.

The morning meeting on the clip begins with an in-joke: my Queen of Grammar overreaction to kids' response that they're "good" when I ask how everyone is. Then it features an addition to our running list of early-spring bird sightings, the introduction of a new estimation jar, my planting a bee in student bonnets about the upcoming bill of rights debate, a poem written by a student who's new to CTL and to poetry, a song, and a couple of silent cheers (the school version of applause). Look for Brian. His school job this month is chart helper, which means he's responsible for holding up the bottoms of oak tag charts so the back row can see the words.

Develop Your Own Morning Meeting

- Logistical details: First, read the resource documents about morning meeting and the guidelines CTL teachers developed to describe what we do and don't want to happen here. A small school—under a hundred students—can conduct friendly whole-school morning meetings. Teachers in larger settings might organize morning meetings by classroom, grade level, or within a wing of the building. The group should be small enough that an individual can speak in a normal voice and be heard by everyone.

- A joyful noise: Create oak tag charts of poems and songs that have the potential to become meaningful to you and your students—topical, seasonal, beautiful, moving, related to science and history topics, or just plain silly. If you have computer-projection ability, you might establish digital collections rather than charts. And consider how morning meeting can provide an occasion to celebrate the musical talents of the staff and kids. Who can play an instrument? Remember that anyone can play a kazoo.

• Incorporate academics: We weave academics into every morning meeting, such as estimation and extrapolation jar problems; "wordy" problems; presentations by teachers or guest experts about science and history topics; current events discussions; descriptions by teachers, students, and parents of holidays of different cultures; Q and A's with local politicians seeking elective office; students' presentations of history and science research projects; a collaborative chart of spring bird sightings; and, during elections, opinion poll, primary contest, and election results.

Tap Resources About Morning Meeting

Since CTL opened in 1990, the faculty has continued to define and refine what we mean by morning meeting. Our best current thinking is represented on the *Systems* DVD, where you'll find:

• Protocols for Morning Meeting

• Agendas for Morning Meeting

• What Doesn't Belong

• Why Everyone Should Sing

• Suggested Songs for Charts

• Suggested Poems for Charts

Protocols for Morning Meeting

- Classroom teachers take turns leading morning meeting. The leader selects or creates poetry charts and song charts and gathers birthday stickers for five days, every five weeks, in this cycle: Nancie, Glenn, Jill, Ted, Helene.
- On Friday afternoon, the teacher who was in the chair takes down and puts away the used charts but makes sure that the school secretary gets the titles and authors of any new songs or poems, to add to the two master lists.
- After selecting the charts for a morning meeting, the leader reviews the lyrics and words, to avoid potential format confusion during the performance and to make sure all the chart pages are there.
- The leader also:
  - Consults with Ted (Can he play a selected song on the guitar?) or cues the iPod.
  - Adds new lyrics and poems to the school's collection, rather than relying on the taste and labor of predecessors.
  - Makes sure the bottom of a chart gets held up, with the help of the student chart assistant, so the back row of children can see the words.
  - Makes sure chart lettering is large enough for everyone to read.
  - Asks his or her group about songs they'd like to sing at morning meeting.
  - Notes that when a poetry chart is marked M, this indicates a poem the student body has attempted to memorize in the past.
  - Provides an introduction to each poem and song—sets it in a personal, social, scientific, historical, or seasonal context.
  - Begins morning meeting by asking for announcements and calls on raised hands; celebrates student, faculty, and staff birthdays with birthday stickers; then poses the question, "Which birthday song would you like?" and, after the singing of that song and "[...] leads the group in asking, "Did you have breakfast in bed?" He or she a[...] gift books from students on behalf of the school.
  - Dismisses students by group to the appropriate content-area rooms.

© 2014 by Nancie Atwell from *Systems to Transform Your Classroom and School.* Ports[...]

Agendas for Morning Meeting

- To start each day together in a happy, predictable way
- To come together as a school and collaborate as a community
- To get to know and learn to respect one another
- To rub shoulders and sit on laps
- To tell others "the important stuff"—for example, what's in the news, animal sightings, friend and personnel sightings outside of school, weather stories and forecasts, family birthdays, a new sibling or cousin or pet, loose or lost teeth, hot topics in current events, and so on
- To read and recite good poems together and get our mouths and minds around wonderful diction, imagery, ideas, and feelings
- To sing and memorize songs together
- To celebrate student and staff birthdays and other special events
- To celebrate individual and school accomplishments
- To introduce visitors to the school
- To welcome and introduce new students by serenading them with Malvina Reynolds' "Move Over and Make Room"
- To teach about historical, religious, and ethnic holidays, events, and traditions
- To accept presents given to the school, including gift books from birthday boys and girls
- To plan community-action projects—for example, a new food pantry drive or humane society collection
- To collect Guatemalan-foster-child dollars and rainforest-acre-adoption pennies
- To take attendance
- To talk and learn about age-appropriate current events in Maine and the U.S.
- To learn from guest teachers or presenters, especially about science, history, and multicultural topics
- To present students' science or history reports or skits
- To solve problems—for example, seek lost items, distribute found items, discuss or role-play playground and other social problems, discuss school jobs, and establish or review school guidelines and procedures
- To create the in-jokes and rituals that give CTL its family feeling
- To propose and plan special events—examples include Pajama Day, Chinese New Year, Gold Rush Day, Leapling Day, Beach Day, Winter Carnival, Colonial Crafts Day, and a Roman feast
- To introduce estimation and extrapolation jars and wordy problems; to discuss the answers and honor the kids who arrived at them
- To learn how to "play" the kazoo
- To develop public voices
- Every five years, to review and revise the CTL Bill of Rights

© 2014 by Nancie Atwell from *Systems to Transform Your Classroom and School.* Portsmouth, NH: Heinemann.

What Doesn't Belong

- Side conversations among students or teachers

- Announcements about new toys or other new possessions, except pets

- Announcements about social occasions (play dates and parties) that don't include everyone in the student's class

- L-o-n-g stories

- Morbid or bloody news *viz.* current events

- Lying down on the pillows or facing the side or back of the room

Why Everyone Should Sing

- *Everybody singing* is what we do.

- Singing helps create community.

- Students may like the song and feel embarrassed or pressured not to sing it if others aren't.

- The teacher and class who chose the song like it.

- If a student can't read the lyrics yet, he or she can learn the chorus from its repetitions.

- The songs are often related to the K–8 science or history curricula or a cultural or religious event; it's cool to sing and learn at the same time.

- Older students who don't sing are teaching younger children not to sing.

Suggested Songs for Charts

"The Anti-Garden Song"	Eric Kilburn
"Apples and Bananas"	Traditional
"Baby Beluga"	Raffi and D. Pike
"Big Fat Fish"	Walkin' Jim Stoltz
"Big Yellow Taxi"	Joni Mitchell
"Birthday"	The Beatles
"Black Socks" (Round)	Traditional
"Boa Constrictor"	Shel Silverstein
"Brown Eyed Girl"	Van Morrison
"Bubble Gum"	Rick Charette
"Build Me Up, Buttercup"	Tony Macaulay and Mike D'Abo
"By the Waters of Babylon" (Round)	Traditional
"Chug-a-Lug-a-Lug"	Traditional
"Circle Game"	Joni Mitchell
"Cows"	Sandra Boynton and Michael Ford
"Dock of the Bay"	Otis Redding and Steve Cropper
"Don't Put Your Finger Up Your Nose"	Barry Louis Polisar
"Do Re Mi"	Richard Rogers and Oscar Hammerstein
"Family Tree"	Tom Chapin and John Forester
"Fields of Gold"	Sting
"The Garden Song"	David Mallett
"Going to the Zoo"	Tom Paxton
"Good Riddance" ("Time of Your Life")	Billy Joe
"Green and Speckled Frogs"	Traditional
"Groundhog"	Pete Seeger
"Habitat"	National Audubon Society
"He's Got the Whole World in His Hands"	Traditional
"Horsey" (Round)	Traditional
"The Hundredth Day of School"	Paul Ippolito
"If I Had a $1,000,000"	Steven Page and Ed Robertson
"If I Should Fall Behind"	Bruce Springsteen
"If You're Happy and You Know It"	Traditional
"I Love Mud"	Rick Charette
"I Love New England Days"	Paul Ippolito
"I Love the Flowers" (Round)	Traditional
"I've Been Working on the Railroad"/ "Down by the Station"	Traditional
"I Walk the Line"	Johnny Cash
"King Tut"	Steve Martin
"L.L. Bean"	Author Unknown

Suggested Poems for Charts

"acorn"	Valerie W…
"Alligator Pie"	Dennis L…
"America"	Walt Wh…
"Anteater"	Valerie W…
"Apple Joys"	Eve Mer…
"The Arrowhead"	Mary Oli…
"Babies"	Ralph Fl…
"Banananananananana"	William …
"The Blue Between"	Kristine …
"Breakers"	Lillian M…
"Brother"	Mary An…
"Cat"	Marilyn S…
"Cat at Rest"	Karla Ku…
"Caterpillar"	Marc Bro…
"Caterpillar Butterfly"	Christina…
"Change"	Charlotte…
"A Cicada Story"	Constance…
Cloud poem (no title)	David M…
"Clouds"	Mary Oli…
"Cold Morning"	Felice H…
"Comma in the Sky"	Aileen Fisher
"Crow Call"	Jane Yolen
"Dandelions"	Valerie Worth
"Daybreak"	Galway Kinnell
"Digging for China"	Richard Wilbur
"A Doe"	Kristine O'Connell George
"Dragonfly"	Marilyn Singer
"Dressing Like a Snake"	Georgia Heard
"The Drum"	Nikki Giovanni
"Eagle Flight"	Georgia Heard
"Edison"	Jean McKinney
"Everytime I Climb a Tree"	David McCord
"Family Photo"	Ralph Fletcher
"Far Away"	Elizabeth Coatsworth
"Fishing"	Martin Steingesser
"Flashlight"	Judith Thurman
"The Floor and the Ceiling"	William Jay Smith
"Fog"	Carl Sandburg
"Fog"	Marilyn Singer
"Forsythia Bush"	Lilian Moore

"BECAUSE THESE ARE
COMMON STANDARDS FOR
BEHAVIOR, WRITTEN AND
AGREED UPON BY K–8
KIDS AND TEACHERS, THE
GREY AREAS OF STUDENT
BEHAVIOR GET CLARIFIED."

3

A Bill of Rights

Talk About It and Reflect

Some students already seem disengaged when they enter the classroom in September. They've learned that school is a place where they won't have voices. Sometimes I sense a comparable feeling of disengagement in teachers at other schools, where their observations and intentions can go unheard. For substantive learning and teaching to take place, students and teachers need to feel recognized as individuals who merit respect and attention.

- Are students and teachers at your school part of regular conversations about rights and rules, expectations for behavior, strategies for meeting the expectations, and recommendations for revision?
- What *are* the expectations for student behavior at your school? In your classroom? Is there consistency and follow-through?
- Do you think students and teachers believe their rights and voices are respected? Does the administration walk the talk of its guidelines for student-to-student, student-to-teacher, and teacher-to-teacher interactions?

Read About CTL's Bill of Rights

By our second year as a school, the teachers recognized we had to codify behavior and expectations beyond "You can't say you can't play." As social dilemmas arose, we needed a whole-school response: expectations for behavior throughout the building and playground. For example, kids of all ages seem to think it's funny to steal another student's lunchbox or book and then hide it. Teachers found we were talking endlessly to students about why it's only funny to the person doing the stealing and hiding.

So we assembled a constitutional convention to create a bill of rights—for example, if you attend this school, how can you expect you'll be treated? What decisions are yours to make? The first suggestion came from Ethan, a kindergartner, who said, "I want to know that my things will be safe." Another student said, "Well, I'd like to be safe. I'd like to be sure that nobody can push or trip me on the playground." Over a series of meetings, the children and teachers established ten rights that individuals could expect would be respected at their school.

Every September, we review the current list of rights someone enjoys as a student and teacher at CTL, and students and teachers plan and role play typical situations in which these might be tested or applied. Then, throughout the school year, we refer to our bill of rights whenever behaviors occur that give us pause. Figure 3.1 represents the most recent version.

We revisit the document every five years. At a series of morning meetings, we debate: "Do we still believe in *this* right? Do two-thirds of us believe in it? Do we want to consider amending it in any way?"

Because these are common standards for behavior, written and agreed upon by K–8 kids and teachers, the grey areas of student behavior get clarified. The importance of mutual respect is codified. And voice, choice, learning, and teaching are elevated and ensured.

It's a bill of rights for children *and* teachers. Teachers also vote on it, suggest ideas to add to it, and discuss problems that have arisen with existing items. Glenn Powers observed that when it comes to the bill of rights, the faculty functions as the executive branch as well as the judiciary. We enforce the document, and sometimes we interpret it or help kids do so. That children helped write it, that they are asked for sincere participation when we revisit it, plays a huge role in lessening problems in behavior. Students buy into it because they help to create it. It's a sign of enormous respect to invite them to reconsider their school's bill of rights. It also keeps it fresh and alive.

Center for Teaching and Learning Bill of Rights

    I.   The right to play with anyone and everyone

   II.   The right to work with anyone and everyone, as the task is appropriate

  III.   The right to work independently, as the task is appropriate

  IV.   The right to be listened to by others

   V.   The right to say what you need to say and think is right

  VI.   The right to be accepted and respected

 VII.   The right to learn

VIII.   The right to teach

  IX.   The right to ask any academic question

   X.   The right to be yourself

  XI.   The right to make your own academic decisions, as the task is appropriate

 XII.   The right to be physically and emotionally safe

XIII.   The right to have your possessions be safe

XIV.   The right to your own beliefs

 XV.   The right to be equal, regardless of your age, sex, gender, race, ethnic background, or religion

XVI.   The right to confidentiality: to have your personal business remain your personal business

Figure 3.1

As songs and poems come and go, the bill of rights is the one oak tag chart that remains on the stand in the room where we hold morning meeting. Every teacher is expected to live it, as a disciplinarian but also as a member of the community. None of us says, "Okay, we've made a list of rules. File it, and let's move on." The bill of rights keeps all of us believing and acting in common.

I urge other teachers and schools to try this—to invite children and teachers to think about what they want their school days to be like, and then to brainstorm, debate, and vote on a list of rights that corresponds with the goals. Then, it's important to return periodically to review and refresh it.

As adults who care about all aspects of our students' lives, CTL teachers sometimes think and talk about how adults at a productive workplace engage with one another. School should be a place where kids can work together in similar ways. They need to learn how to grow as individuals and as members of a team.

Since there's only one class at each grade level, I worried when we started the school about how we'd deal with students in the same grade who didn't get on together. But then I thought about how adults at work don't change their colleagues at the end of every year. Instead, we figure out how to get along and get the job done, sometimes with the help of others. Another benefit of being a student at CTL is that children learn how to adapt to others, because teachers and the bill of rights help kids with different personalities and perspectives accept one another.

I've learned it's both realistic and healthy to keep groups of children together from year to year, work with them on resolving social difficulties, and watch them learn to support— even love—one another. Students come to trust that every September they'll rejoin individuals they have learned to work and play with, friends who own, in common, a bill of their rights.

Watch Day One of a Constitutional Convention

As you view the start of a debate that played out over a week of morning meetings, notice how asking kids to focus on positive outcomes helps them think and talk as their best selves: thoughtful, productive, and considerate. Also, observe how there's no hidden teacher agenda. Students' ideas and voices are central and crucial. Teachers listen, paraphrase, and respond, while still acting as the adults in the room and the ultimate authorities.

And watch the older kids. Nearing the end of their careers at CTL, they consider the bill of rights from new perspectives. The best revisions to ours have been suggested by students in grades seven and eight, who recognize how the document has—and hasn't—functioned for them as learners and individuals, as they envision how they want the school to carry on after they're gone.

Hold Your Own Constitutional Convention

- Over a period of several days or a week, discuss with students and teachers the rights you believe people should enjoy in a good school, the environment in which a student learns best, and the conditions in which a teacher best teaches. Debate, amend, vote, and adopt the principles that achieve a two-thirds majority.
- Plan how you'll revisit your bill of rights, and create periodic opportunities to discuss how children and grown-ups at your school are learning, teaching, and treating one another.

Tap Resources About School and Classroom Culture

The documents listed below provide a fleshed-out foundation for expectations for student and teacher behavior at CTL. Each appears in our faculty handbook and is included on the *Systems* DVD. Feel free to use them as inspiration in creating your own faculty handbook.

- The Gestalt: Characteristics of CTL Teachers
- Expectations for Discipline and Behavior
- Relationships with Students

The Gestalt: Characteristics of CTL Teachers

Professional Traits

- Teachers pay attention to individual students—the needs, goals, strengths, problems, talents, and interests of each boy and girl.
- Teachers are responsible to students and their parents. We determine to do our best by every child.
- Teachers demonstrate passion for the topics, concepts, and skills we teach.
- Teachers prepare intensely, including the acquisition of worthwhile, essential knowledge and skills.
- Teachers acknowledge that teaching and learning are processes that involve both success and failure.
- Teachers are interested in new ideas and discovering how something might be done better . . .
- . . . but also conserve methods, sticking with ideas, systems, approaches, and curricula that work.
- Teachers demonstrate consistency and follow-through: the ability to stay the course, bring closure, and help students feel a sense of accomplishment.
- Teachers understand the importance of authentic learning experiences.
- Teachers can reveal the theory behind an activity—explain why we're teaching in a certain way or asking kids to act as they do, in terms of child development, concept development, and development of skills.
- Teachers are flexible: we can shift course when something isn't working in our teaching.
- Teachers notice revealing specifics, the details that make CTL work institutionally, interpersonally, and academically.
- Teachers are willing to ask questions when uncertain and to seek help when stuck.
- Teachers are proactive: What do I need to try to understand? What's really going on here? What needs to happen next? How can I help others?
- Teachers debate ideas, listen to colleagues, and compromise.
- Teachers are civil and professional, even when disagreeing.
- Teachers demonstrate professional curiosity and scholarship: we read professional texts, attend conferences, conduct research, and engage in continuous professional growth.

Collegiality

- Teachers pitch in without being asked; we view the curriculum, building, school resources, and all the students as our shared responsibility.
- Teachers are generous: we share ideas, methods, materials, resources, and plans.
- Teachers give one another credit, acknowledge colleagues' authorship (e.g., an adapted form should include a credit to its creator), and express gratitude for assistance and inspiration.
- Teachers ask the previous year's teacher questions about incoming students' strengths and challenges.
- Teachers share observations with the previous year's teacher about incoming students' strengths and challenges.

Expectations for Discipline and Behavior

- The CTL Bill of Rights is the school's benchmark for student and teacher behavior.
- Teachers frame discussions with students about appropriate behavior in terms of the cultural mores of the school: "This is the way we do things here." "Our Bill of Rights says...."
- The focus of discipline at CTL is on inclusivity, community, and productivity.
- Teachers insist on respect for other people and their property, plus the school's.
- Teachers don't raise our voices.
- Teachers and students respond to and use the CTL *quiet* gesture: right hand on left shoulder.
- Hand raising is expected, and talking isn't permitted when someone else has the floor.
- Teachers find natural consequences for student misbehavior—examples include sitting out of the group, cleaning up a mess, and staying in at recess if homework isn't done.
- Teachers don't blanket accuse or punish groups, that is, remonstrate with the entire class for the behavior of some of its members or withhold an opportunity from children because of the actions of a few.
- "You can't say you can't play" (Vivian Paley) all teachers. Teachers help students role-pla meeting or in our classes.
- K–6 kids wear inside shoes or slippers inside
- Students put away materials and equipmen
- Students in grades 1–8 perform their assign school.
- Each teacher of grades 1–8 makes sure his
- At lunchtime, teachers ensure that each stu placemat, sits with the group, and buses his
- No gum chewing is allowed in the building
- Hats aren't worn in the building. Clothing
- Students may not sell candy, gum, or cooki
- There is no seat saving or line saving.

Relationships with Students

- Teachers know the names of all CTL students, K–8.
- Teachers like—if not love—our kids and try to care about them as good parents would.
- Teachers are affectionate and hands-on, including hugs or, for discipline, a hand on a shoulder.
- There is no labeling of students as types: kids are seen and discussed by teachers as individuals.
- Teachers don't encourage competition. We establish conditions for engagement, achievement, collaboration, and individual goal setting.
- Teachers begin by assuming that students are doing the best they can and that it's our job to help each student build on his or her best.
- Teachers recognize that children will make mistakes and misbehave. We regard each day as a fresh chance for everyone.
- Teachers don't yell at children. We recognize the power of a low, intense voice and a piercing gaze.
- Teachers are steady and reliable—no bad moods, power trips, or arbitrary rules or punishments.
- Teachers demonstrate excitement about what we're teaching and asking kids to learn.
- If a teacher has favorite students, no one can tell who they are.
- If there's a student toward whom a teacher feels less than warm, no one can tell that either.

"There is no shortcut to reading proficiency—no core program or digital platform that's going to do it."

4

Reading Workshop

Talk About It and Reflect

- Describe your ideal reader. What are his or her behaviors? Attitudes? Habits? Responses? Appreciations? Understandings?
- What do you ask of students that will help them grow up to become your ideal reader?
- How much time, over the course of a week, do you estimate your students spend reading books?
- What strategies do they have for selecting books for themselves?
- How, and when, do you and your students talk about books you love?

Read About Reading Workshop

The only way for students to become good readers is to read books, lots of them. There is no shortcut to reading proficiency—no core program or digital platform that's going to do it. Kids need multiple, sustained experiences with books they love, because these will compel them to read.

Reading workshop has the same structure in every classroom, K–8. It begins with the children gathered in a circle around their teacher for a minilesson. This might be a discussion of a genre, literary feature, author, or illustrator; a booktalk, bookwalk, or read-aloud; or, in the primary grades, a guided reading lesson or the introduction of a decoding strategy. The minilesson is followed by time for individuals to read independently while the teacher meets with them about what they're reading, why they're reading it, and how.

CTL students can anticipate from year to year what their reading program will look like. From kindergarten through eighth grade, they'll choose their books from collections selected by their teachers and stored in libraries appropriate to students of particular ages and levels of development. Every child has a reading folder with a record form inside to keep track of the titles he or she finishes or abandons over the course of the year. They engage full bore, from the first day of school, as people who choose books and who read and talk about them, and they develop stamina, habits, fluency, vocabulary, preferences, and literary criteria.

In his book *Outliers* (2008), Malcolm Gladwell writes about the ten thousand hours of committed practice that are required for someone to become an expert at something. In a workshop, between the reading children do at school every day and the thirty minutes of reading their teachers require at home every night, our students achieve that level of experience because it involves books they choose and love.

Starting in kindergarten, teachers assign the most important homework of all: to read or be read to every night for half an hour. We provide our K–4 kids with overnight book bags,

sewn by parent volunteers in bright, hard-to-ignore fabrics, to transport titles home at night and back to school the next morning. "Reading: How Parents Can Help," the longest section in the school's parent handbook, explains why reading is priority homework and provides suggestions for how parents can support beginning readers. I've included it in the *Systems* DVD for you to inspire the parents of your students.

Claire retrieves her reading folder to record a book.

Jill's Group's Display of Books They Love

Any K–6 teacher who is responsible for the whole gamut of subjects will acknowledge that his or her number one goal is for students to be reading well by June. It's essential for kids to be at least on grade level, because so much follows from that—the students who read the most and best tend to do well in math, science, and history, too. A benefit for reading workshop teachers is that we see the results. Our kids leap into literacy.

I remember a note I received from a mother of a first grader who joked it had become intolerable to ride in the car with her daughter because all she wanted to do was read street signs out loud: "Reny's Underground." "Brackett's Market." "Twenty-five miles per hour." "Trucks: release brakes here." Gracie's introduction to literacy was wonderful children's literature and lots of conversations with teachers Helene and Ted about lots of books, plus the stories she read and heard read aloud at home.

And I recall Mike, a student who enrolled at CTL as a seventh grader. He announced he had never read a book, and he catalogued the strategies he used to avoid reading— hiding an electronic game behind the core program anthology, copying other kids' homework, and listening in on discussions to glean

Nancie's Group's Display of Books They Love

Ted's Group's Display of Books They Love

the gist of a story. That September, for his benefit, I conducted booktalks about sure-fire novels and nonfiction titles for adolescent boys.

A booktalk is like a commercial: synopsize the plot, introduce the main character, tell what his or her problem or conflict is, and end on a cliffhanger. This way, if a student wants to find out what happens, he or she has to read the book.

Every child loves a good story. Mike, and students like him, don't understand that by reading books they get to live inside great stories, alongside characters they'll never forget. By June, Mike had read thirty-six books—many of them titles he practically ripped out of my hands at the ends of booktalks because he was so curious to find out what happened next. Stories fuel literacy. If we deny children stories, we deny them the prime motivation for engaging as readers, the development of lifelong reading habits, and the possibility of literary relationships, starting with those they form with classmates.

A social network blooms in reading workshops as kids recommend titles to one another, engage in fierce arguments about literary worth, ask peers if a book gets better, trade books, and talk about plot developments, characters, and themes they love. None of this talk—which happens at the beginning and end of class, during lunch and recess, and on the bus—is orchestrated by teachers. Kids who choose and read books talk about them just as book-loving adults do. A crucial way that Mike segued into his new peer group at CTL was within a shared context of stories he and other boys had experienced vicariously and gabbed about as if the characters were friends. At the same time, he demonstrated an extraordinary bump in his reading proficiency as a result of all that practice.

This doesn't mean that teachers don't play a role in the love-of-books phenomenon. We set the tone. A teacher's uninhibited pleasure in books, characters, and authors, expressed in booktalks and conversations with individual readers, is infectious. Our most powerful tool as reading teachers is great stories. We need to read them, express enthusiasm about them, and give kids opportunities to be enthusiastic, too. CTL readers are uninhibited because their teachers are. It's another part of the school culture: we love books here.

Like Mike, students who don't have regular, consistent access to trade books and time to choose and read them—who complete exercises from a core reading program, grind along in textbooks, or pretend along with the class novel—can fake it in more ways than we can imagine. I know, because it's what I did. During my high school years, I read just one of the assigned novels; with the others, I consulted CliffsNotes or fed on lectures and discussions. And I was a so-called good reader. I could decode anything.

Teachers know, and test scores show, that students can become adequate decoders by around third grade but never enter the reading zone. These are kids who don't get lost in books. They never have life-enhancing, vicarious experiences with characters. They can't name favorite titles, authors, or genres; nor do the themes they glean from books inform their view of the world beyond the classroom.

We must invite kids into stories they select as often and for as long as possible. Because workshop teachers check in with our kids every day during independent reading time, we recognize immediately when a reader is engaged and when he isn't. When Mike wasn't, I encouraged him to abandon the book, review the list of "someday" titles that students of grades 3–8 keep in response to intriguing booktalks, and look for a story he could love, would inhale, and that might contribute another handful of happy hours toward that goal of ten thousand.

Watch Warm-Ups, Minilessons, and Conferences

The clip opens with booktalks by me, two seventh graders, and a third grader. The kids reveal just enough about plot, character, genre, and theme to whet a reader's interest without giving away the ending. Note the ratings system we use as shorthand for excellence. Our kids don't booktalk titles they rate lower than a nine out of ten; otherwise that book is going to sit on the shelf for the rest of the school year. Unless it's a new title we're introducing for someone in the group to volunteer to preview, teachers only booktalk titles we think particular students in our class will love. We read a lot of books.

Helene's first reading minilesson is her daily morning message, a CLOZE exercise that invites kindergartners to predict the words she omitted. The emphasis is on making sense: here, semantic cues are the focus.

Glenn's minilesson, about the function of secondary characters in fiction, is based on a summary of the notes his fifth and sixth graders made in the previous reader's roundtable (a subject of Chapter 7). The kids' discussion was rich and valuable, so Glenn captures and formalizes its key points and distributes them to students to tape into their writing-reading handbooks and highlight. Their literary theories get preserved, reviewed, and made available for future reference. Glenn and I follow this routine—type it up and tape it in—a lot. When they're not captured, it's easy for lessons to evaporate. Glenn's summary of his kids' discoveries about secondary characters is included on the *Systems* DVD.

In another reading minilesson, Helene introduces a poem. The focus here is on new sight words—words that don't conform to phonetic generalizations. Notice how, by the end of April, the kindergartners are reading with fluency and expression. The role of poetry in captivating and teaching beginning readers is another subject of Chapter 7.

Jill's minilesson is a response to an issue that arose in her students' evaluation conferences: inconsistencies in their definitions of the three kinds of books, holidays, just rights, and challenges. Her purpose is to review the guidelines that point her students to books appropriate to their skill levels and get her class back on common ground.

You'll see five quick reading conferences. Notice how teachers move among students as they read, record titles of books and the page numbers kids are on, ask questions about choice and content and process, confirm what kids are doing, and give advice.

One note: in his conference with Teagan, Glenn talks about "interviewing" books. This is the term his kids use to describe the range of considerations that come into play when an intentional reader decides to read—or not read—a particular title.

Develop Your Own Reading Workshop

- Do whatever it takes to make reading inviting, enjoyable, and meaningful. This means student access to books that tell great stories, freedom of choice, time to read, and encouragement and information along the way. Acknowledge that it's engaged practice that makes readers, and try to carve out time every day for your students to curl up with books.

- Build a classroom library of compelling titles. I started by borrowing collections from my school library and then signed titles out to individual kids. Today, CTL students browse in classroom libraries that offer a minimum of thirty titles per reader. The books they nominate as sure-fire invitations to other kids appear on our school website, www.c-t-l.org, on the *kids recommend* page; students update the lists three times a year. And, of course, teachers need to get and keep our own feet wet as readers of children's and young adult literature.

- Keep track of the books students borrow. We staple together a packet of 4" × 6" cards for each child, write his or her name on it, and store the cards on a bookshelf in the class library. When a student borrows a book, he or she writes its title on the top card; when the book is returned, the teacher draws a line through the title and initials it. This system is simple, and it works. We lose few books, and when someone is looking for a title, it's easy to flip through the cards to identify its borrower.

Sophia signs out her next book selection.

- Remember that the teacher's main role in reading workshop is to talk with readers. Meet with individuals and engage in quiet conversations about what they're reading, how they're reading it, what they're understanding and noticing, whether they're happy or struggling, and what they might read next. Speak in minilessons to the whole group about decoding strategies in K–2 and, in K–8, reading workshop routines, particular titles, authors and illustrators, genres, literary elements, and approaches to selecting, reading, abandoning, and criticizing books.

- In grades K–2, conduct bookwalks: turn pages and display the illustrations from works of children's literature as you tell a bit about the story and ask for students' observations and predictions. In grades K–8, conduct booktalks—sales pitches about titles you love and think your students will, too—and invite kids to present booktalks about their beloved titles. Help students create a place to record titles that sound intriguing to them, so they can make plans as readers. Our kids of grades 3–8 maintain writing-reading handbooks—spiral notebooks in which they capture information presented in minilessons. Each child sets aside two pages in his or her handbook for "someday titles." Before a booktalk, Jill, Glenn, and I ask our kids to turn to their someday pages and be ready to add to their lists if a recommendation so moves them.

Tap Resources About Reading Workshop

There are many published resources for K–8 teachers new to reading workshop or looking to refine their practice. For teachers of grades 5–8, I've written two books, *In the Middle* (Heinemann) and *The Reading Zone* (Scholastic). Heinemann also produced *Reading in the Middle*, a demonstration video of my grades 7–8 reading workshop.

Helene Coffin's book *Every Child a Reader: Month by Month Lessons to Teach Beginning Reading* (Scholastic) describes in detail how she weaves poetry into her kindergarten reading workshop at CTL so that, by June, every child is not only adept at decoding, but also an enthusiastic reader. Helene and I also recommend, for primary-grade teachers, *The Early Detection of Reading Difficulties, Third Edition*, by Marie M. Clay (Heinemann) and *Word Matters: Teaching Phonics and Spelling in the Reading/Writing Classroom* by Irene Fountas and Gay Su Pinnell (Heinemann).

At the intermediate level, we appreciate *Day-to-Day Assessment in the Reading Workshop: Making Informed Instructional Decisions in Grades 3–6* (Scholastic) and *Still Learning to Read* (Stenhouse), both by Franki Sibberson, as well as her collaboration with Karen Szymusiak and Lisa Koch, *Beyond Leveled Books: Supporting Early and Transitional Readers in Grades 5–8* (Stenhouse).

Forthcoming from Stenhouse is *Reader's Roundtable: Conversations at the Core of a Reading Classroom* by Glenn Powers, which describes his powerful innovation in the reading workshop: weekly discussions among a whole class of students about what they notice in individual books about literary and genre features, themes, narrative structures, and other authorial choices.

The CTL website, www.c-t-l.org, features not only titles that our students rate as surefire nines and tens, but also reviews of intermediate and young adult titles, written by the fifth through eighth graders.

Feel free to adapt or adopt the documents listed below for reading workshops in your classroom or school, all provided on the *Systems* DVD:

- Sample Reading Record, Grade 3 (Nicco)
- Sample Reading Record, Grade 7 (Noah)
- Sample List of Someday Titles, Grade 3 (Katie)
- Sample List of Someday Titles, Grade 8 (Helena)
- Reading: How Parents Can Help
- Expectations for Reading Workshop, Gr. 1–2
- Expectations for Reading Workshop, Gr. 3–4
- Expectations for Reading Workshop, Gr. 7–8
- Rules for Reading Workshop, Gr. 7–8

Books I'd Like to read Someday   Katie

1. The Chocolate Touch ☑
2. The Runaway Dolls ☐
3. Pie ☐
4. Toys go out ☑
5. Ivy + Bean Bound to be Bad ☑
6. "   "   Break the fossil re
7. "   "   And The ghost Aho
8. ESIO Trot ☑
9. Christmas After All ☐
10. Matilda ☑

Expectations for Reading Workshop, Grades 7–8

(Nancie Atwell)

- Read as much as you can as joyfully as you can. Practice with pleasure and commitment. Remember Malcolm Gladwell's ten thousand hours as the route to expertise.

- Read at home for at least a half an hour every day, seven days a week, all year long.

- Find books, authors, subjects, genres, and themes that matter to who you are now, who you were, and who you might become.

- Try new books, authors, subjects, genres, and themes. Expand your literary experience, knowledge, and appreciation.

- On the Someday pages in your writing-reading handbook, keep a running list of titles and authors you'd like to try, especially in response to booktalks and recommendations.

- Recognize that a book represents a writer's ideas and the choices he or she made. Understand that you can step back from a story, after you've finished living inside it, and notice and discuss the author's decisions.

- Use the critical vocabulary you already know and the terms I teach you when you talk and write about literature.

- Write a letter-essay every three weeks about what you noticed and appreciated about one book you recently finished. Go back into the book as a critic and think on paper about what the author did, how the author wrote, what worked, what needs more work, how the book made you think and feel, and its *themes*—the ideas about life that you came away with.

- Recognize that readers take different stances in relation to different kinds of texts. Reading a novel is different from a poem, a chapter in a history book, a newspaper editorial, a word problem in math, or the instructions for assembling a new bicycle.

- Develop and articulate your own criteria for selecting and abandoning books.

- Each trimester, work toward significant, relevant goals for yourself as a reader.

...ard engaging and
...shop. Use it to find
...ur imagination, find
...ems and experiences you
...r soul, consider how
...dge and insights, wonder,

...rtsmouth, NH: Heinemann.

Sample Reading Record, Grade 3 (Nicco)

Jill Cotta
Center for Teaching and Learning

READING RECORD   Name _Nicco – 3_

Title	Author	Date Started	Date Finished	Genre	H/JR/C
5 novels	Daniel Pinkwater	9-7	9-9	Fiction	J R
Eragon	Christopher Padini	9/9	9-11	Fantasy	J R
Eldest	C.P.	9-11	9-13	Fantasy	J R
Brisingr	C.P.	9-13	9-15	Fantasy	J R
The Neddiad	Daniel Pinkwater	9-15	9-19	Fiction	J R
The Yggysev	Daniel Pinkwater	9-19	9-27	Fiction	J R
Mister Monday	Garth Nix	9-27	10-3	Mystery	J R
Grim Tuesday	Garth Nix	10-3	10-7	Mystery	J R
Drowned Wednesday	Garth Nix	10-7	10-10	Mystery	J R
Sir Thursday	Garth Nix	10-10	10-15	Mystery	J R
Lady Friday	Garth Nix	10-15	10-20	Mystery	J R
Superior saturday	Garth Nix	10-20	11-1	Mystery	J R
Fablehaven	Brandon Mull	11-1	11-7	Fantasy	J R
Fablehaven 2	Brandon Mull	11-7	11-10	Fantasy	J R
Fablehaven 3	Brandon Mull	11-10	11-13	Fantasy	J R
The Gravity Keeper	Simon Bloom	11-13	11-16	Fantasy	J R

Rules for Reading Workshop, Grades 7–8

(Nancie Atwell)

1. You must read a book. Magazines and newspapers can't provide the sustained chunks of text you need to practice reading and develop fluency. More importantly, they won't help you discover who you are as a reader of books.

2. Don't continue to read a book you're not enjoying. Don't waste time with a title you don't like, when there are so many great stories waiting for you—*unless* you decide to finish a bad book so you can criticize it in a letter-essay. Do develop your own criteria for abandoning books—for example, how many pages will you give an author to intrigue or engage you?

3. If you don't like your book, find another. Check out the books-we-love display. Look at your list of Someday titles. Browse our shelves. Interview books or ask me or a friend for a recommendation.

4. It's more than all right to reread a book you love. This is something good readers do.

5. It's okay to skim or skip parts of a story if you get bored or stuck: good readers do this, too.

6. On the form inside your reading folder, record the **title** of every book you finish or abandon, its specific **genre**, the **author**, the **date**, and your **rating** of the writing, 1–10. Use the number column on the left to keep track of the books you finish. Collect data about your reading, look for patterns, and take satisfaction in your accomplishments and discoveries.

7. Understand that reading is thinking. Do nothing that distracts your friends from the reading zone: don't put your words into their brains as they're trying to enter the worlds of their books. When you talk with me about your book, *whisper*.

8. Take care of our books. Sign out on your cards every o[...]
   me—I'll draw a line through the title and initial it. Res[...]
   alphabetically by the author's last name. Or, if it's a bo[...]
   collection. Then return your card packet to the box.

9. Read the whole time.

10. Read as well, as much, and as happily as you can.

Sample Reading Record, Grade 7 (Noah)

Nancie Atwell
Center for Teaching and Learning

Reading Record for NOAH - 7

#	TITLE	GENRE	AUTHOR	DATE FINISHED	DATE ABANDONED	RATING
1	The White Tiger	CRF	Aravind Adiga	9/11		10
2	The Reapers Are the Angels	horror	Alden Bell	9/16		9
3	A Clockwork Orange	dystopian sci-fi	Anthony Burgess	9/20		9
4	About a Boy	CRF	Nick Hornby	9/25		10
5	Lord of the Flies	classic	William Golding	9/30		9
6	Rebecca	mystery	Daphne Du Maurier	10/13		7.5
7	Marching Powder	journalism	Rusty Young	10/20		10
8	The English Patient	historical fiction	Michael Ondaatje	11/1		10
9	City of Thieves	historical thriller	David Benioff	11/7		10
10	Give a Boy a Gun	CRF	Todd Strasser	11/13		9
11	Ant Farm	humor	Simon Rich	11/15		10
	In Cold Blood	journalism	Truman Capote		11/17	
12	Without Feathers	humor	Woody Allen	11/24		9
13	Fahrenheit 451	dystopian sci-fi	Ray Bradbury	11/30		9
14	Humor	humor	Dick Ziegler	12/9		8.5
15	One Flew Over the Cuckoo's Nest	CRF	Ken Kesey	12/20		8.5
16	Stuck in Neutral	CRF	Terry Trueman	1/8		9.5
17	I am the Messenger	CRF	Markus Zusak	1/15		10
18	Slam	CRF	Nick Hornby	1/20		10
19	The Glass Castle	memoir	Jeanette Walls	1/25		10
20	Breaking Night	memoir	Liz Murray	1/31		10
21	The Round House	CRF	Louise Erdrich	2/10		9
	Cold Mountain	historical fiction	Charles Frasier		2/12	
22	Be More Chill	sci fi	Ned Vizzini	2/20		10

"To invite children to develop as writers in the context of ideas that compel them, that they desire to write about, is the ideal."

5

Writing Workshop

Talk About It and Reflect

- What do you want your students to understand about good writing, its purposes and qualities? What do you hope they'll be able to do as writers when they leave your classroom? Your school?

- How often do your students write? What genres do they produce? Why these? What are the sources for the lessons you teach about writing? How do you support individual students as they plan, draft, revise, and edit their writing?

- When do your students see, read, or discuss demonstrations of your writing?

- How do your students show that their writing matters to them? How do you show your students that their writing matters to you?

Read About Writing Workshop

Our kids write well, K–8. We were hugely influenced by the research of Donald Graves, starting with the amount of time students need to engage in writing in order to grow as writers: at least three days a week for at least forty-five minutes at a shot. In early discussions about

CTL's curriculum, when the faculty determined that writing and reading workshop would be *the* English program, we decided that writing instruction would take place at least four days a week, from between forty-five minutes and an hour and fifteen minutes. As with reading, child writers need consistent practice. Writing development is a slow-growth process, more like mathematics than any other subject, in terms of learning and reviewing the conventions and concepts, failing and succeeding, and practicing, practicing, practicing.

Intrigued, then convinced, by the work of Don Graves and his colleague Donald Murray, we invited children to decide what to write about. Desire and purpose make all the difference between writing as an exercise and genuine self-expression. While Helene's kindergartners are writing about their moms, sleds, and hermit crabs, my middle schoolers are addressing such topics as prejudice and stereotyping, books they've read and films they've viewed, natural phenomena they've observed, local nonprofits they believe deserve support, and the impact of personal experiences on their growing up. It's a developmental range that's compelled by children who believe "I have a voice as a writer, and this is a worthwhile subject for me to address." If stories are the foundation of reading workshop, self-expression is the foundation of writing workshop.

Each teacher organizes his or her writing workshop as a series of genre studies. This allows us to teach minilessons that are relevant to every writer and help children build expertise from one kind of writing to another. Figure 5.1 shows the genres we teach across the two years our kids are with each of us, apart from their single year in kindergarten with Helene. These genre lists are significant: they were created by teachers who know writing and know their kids.

Three genres cut across grade levels at CTL: free-verse poetry, memoirs, and gifts of writing. The last are poems and stories that children write to express love and appreciation for moms, dads, grandparents, and others on the winter holidays, Valentine's Day, Mother's Day, Father's Day, and friend and family birthdays. Gifts of writing are stunning examples of self-expression, purposeful and lasting. They also happen to be an effective public-relations scheme in promoting parental support for writing workshop.

On the genre list we characterize memoirs as *simple* or *reflective*, to differentiate younger children's narratives about events in their lives from older students' explorations of the significance of experiences—the themes, patterns, and meanings that emerge.

Poems appear on every teacher's list because we believe poetry is the essential genre in a K–8 writing curriculum. Every lesson we want to teach about effective writing is writ large here, from the need for concrete specifics, reflection, evidence and information, and meaning to the power of tone, stance, sensory imagery, sound effects, figurative language, compression,

Genres Taught in CTL's Writing Workshops

K *(Helene Coffin)*

- poetry
- simple memoirs
- alphabet books
- counting books
- lists
- labels
- cards
- thank-you and get-well letters
- gifts of writing

1–2 *(Ted DeMille)*

- poetry
- simple memoirs
- lists
- invitations
- thank-you and other friendly letters
- informational booklets
- books to know and be known (about children's lives and families)
- letters to authors
- fairy tales
- picture books
- simple fiction
- autobiographies
- biographies
- gifts of writing

3–4 *(Jill Cotta)*

- poetry
- simple memoirs
- friendly letters
- thank-you, get-well, and condolence letters
- letters to authors
- short stories
- picture books
- book reviews
- personal essays and reports
- peer biographies
- gifts of writing

(Note: in reading workshop, regular letters about books)

5–6 *(Glenn Powers)*

- poetry
- memoirs (simple and reflective)
- various short fiction genres
- Letters about Literature (Library of Congress competition)
- letters of change, i.e., complaint or persuasion
- movie reviews, plus book reviews for the CTL blog
- dramatic monologues
- gifts of writing

(Note: in reading workshop, regular literary letters)

7–8 *(Nancie Atwell)*

- poetry
- reflective memoirs
- microfiction
- movie and television program reviews, plus book reviews for the CTL blog
- essays
- profiles
- advocacy journalism
- parodies
- thank-you, get-well, and condolence letters
- graduation speeches
- gifts of writing

(Note: in reading workshop, regular letter-essays about literature)

Figure 5.1

and careful diction. Free verse is a generous, versatile genre: its subjects are limitless. And it's a compact genre. It's possible for a student to complete three or four poems during the first weeks of school—to experience a complete writing process that many times by the beginning of October. Apart from Helene, all the CTL teachers launch writing workshop in September with a genre study that explores the power of free verse. No genre is more practical in developing purpose, voice, and theme.

Within every genre study, students develop the topics and projects they wish to address. Concerned teachers from other schools will sometimes pose a variation on the question, "I have a student who's crazy about *Star Wars*. All he wants to do is write about *Star Wars*. What should I do?" Writing workshops that are organized as genre studies allow students to develop niches as writers.

I am a niche writer—all I write about is education. It's my *Star Wars*. Some of my students have grown up to write professionally about their middle-school niches: pop music, environmental issues, literature, poetry, even catalog copy about Coach handbags. I ask teachers not to discourage kids from writing again and again about the same topic but instead to introduce literary genres. A student might conduct original research about the guitar, write poems about playing the guitar, and compose a memoir about the role of the guitar in shaping his identity. When writing is viewed as self-expression, kids who are skilled at it can take it as a tool into the rest of their lives.

We know that the more successful an adult is—the higher he or she rises in the hierarchy of a profession—the more writing the job requires. Writing is a skill that's prized. To invite children to develop as writers in the context of ideas that compel them, that they desire to write about, is the ideal. Practice and purpose go hand in hand, and we answer for every child the question, "Why would anybody want to write?" The answer is *because I have this story to tell, this feeling to capture, this phenomenon that needs exploring, this cause that requires my powers of persuasion, and I'm itching to get to it.*

Another concern teachers voice about writing workshop involves revision: their students don't. Our response is, have they seen it? I can't arrange for a professional poet, a Billy Collins or a Nikki Giovanni, to come to my classroom and show kids what they do when they draft and revise their fantastic poems. Chances are, if students are going to observe an adult messing about on the page, it's going to be their teacher. We need to take responsibility for demonstrating to students how an adult thinks, rethinks, and makes meaning on the page.

I save weeks of instructional time each fall because I give my class a piece of my writing—photocopies of the final version along with each messy page of draft. I ask them to study it in search of questions about the choices and changes I made. Then they ask their questions, I answer them, and they collaborate on a list of things one writer, their teacher, thinks about and does when trying to write a good poem. See Figure 5.2 for an example.

After forty years of teaching, I still curl my toes when I show students a piece of my writing. But what they get from a teacher demonstration is worth days of lessons and explanations. They get to observe all the unpredictable yet focused behaviors we call writing process—from the need to draft double-spaced to create room for revision, to all the different ways someone can change his or her mind on the page, to the importance of being picky about verbs, to how titles mostly come last, after the writer has discovered what a piece of writing is really about. Teachers need to get over it. We only have to write *a little bit better than they do* for our students to learn from our demonstrations. All of my colleagues use their writing in minilessons, to significant effect.

Donald Graves determined that a successful writing class has a predictable structure. The workshop starts with a whole-group minilesson. Next, the teacher conducts a status-of-the-class conference, in which we poll writers about their plans for independent writing time, record their answers, and hold children accountable. Then individuals write—or, in the case of kindergartners in the fall, begin to learn to write by telling and drawing their stories—and their teachers move from student to student to show kids how to improve their writing.

Students come to rely on the routines of the workshop. They think about their writing when they're not writing, because they know that tomorrow will bring an occasion to settle in and draft. And they count on it that, at the start of class, their teacher will show or tell them something useful—about workshop procedures, techniques of craft, topic development, genre features, revision strategies, or the conventions of edited American English, without a work-sheet or core program in sight.

The materials for writing workshop are consistent, K–8. Every student has two folders, one for writing in process and one for finished work. Finished writing—the final copy and all its pages of plans and drafts—stays on file at school all year. Because writing is such a slow-growth process, teachers and students need access to collections of it, so we can look for evidence of growth over time.

Teachers set up individual hanging folders in crates or file-cabinet drawers to store the finished writing folders. Each contains a form on which the writer records the titles, genres, and

Some Things a Poet Does When Trying to Write a Good Poem

- Finds a topic that matters, that calls his or her name
- Writes off-the-page to generate ideas, details, a form, sensory verbs, a so what?, and so forth, as well as to create enough momentum to start drafting in the first place
- Writes off-the-page on the poem itself—in the margins—to capture words and ideas that otherwise would get lost and to brainstorm new possibilities
- Drafts double-spaced, so there's room to change his or her mind and to write off-the-page
- Drafts in lines and stanzas
- Experiments with form—the number of lines in each stanza or how stanzas will begin or end
- Focuses on verbs: are they sensory? Especially: are they visual?
- Draws a line when stuck during drafting, keeps going, and comes back later to fill it in
- Consults a thesaurus to find a sensory word or one that will create alliteration or assonance

- Tries to avoid adverbs and to stick with strong verbs
- Envisions sensory images and tries to find the words for them
- Uses repetition to move the poem and create cadence
- Listens for and deletes ineffective repetition
- Rereads a *lot*—the whole poem and individual lines and stanzas—while drafting
- Experiments with punctuation and the voice/tone/mood it can convey
- Hunts for weak words
- Brainstorms lists of strong words to replace a weak one
- Draws a wavy line under "clunky" words or phrases
- Indicates spelling uncertainties along the way by circling them
- Uses === to create new stanzas and / to create new lines
- Starts a new stanza when writing about a new idea
- Listens to the poem and revises it in pursuit of rhythm, a good sound

Figure 5.2

- Pushes for a *so what?* while drafting and revising
- Cuts language to the bone: deletes anything a smart reader doesn't need, that doesn't make the poem stronger, or that isn't specific and concrete
- Gut-checks at the single-word level: is each word the right one?
- Sweats the conclusion: generates and experiments with different ways to end a poem, because this is the most important part, where the deepest meaning or so what? is found
- Thinks about the poem when not working on it—walks away and lets the draft of the poem simmer

- Comes back, after a break, with a fresh perspective
- Brainstorms potential titles when the poem is done or close to it, in search of one that's not a label and that intrigues, invites, *and* fits the whole poem
- Understands that almost nothing in a good poem is an accident or a gift. Good writing is thinking and rethinking on paper: generating options, making choices, and being open to the surprises that occur along the way

Figure 5.2 *continued*

dates of his or her completed pieces. Another K–8 commonality is an individualized proofreading list of the conventions of usage, format, and spelling that a teacher has asked a child to incorporate into his or her writing. Students clip their proofreading lists in the brass fasteners of their writing-in-process folders.

The tone of writing workshop is also consistent across grades. After a deliberate minilesson, one that's designed to engage children and convey practical advice, the workshop is quiet. We carve out a contemplative space where we expect students to think and behave as writers. As we move among them and confer, we do so with soft voices. It's a pleasure and a privilege for CTL teachers to perch alongside children, read and listen to their emerging ideas, and teach them what we've learned about how to compose a poem, a story, an essay, a life.

Watch Warm-Ups, Minilessons, and Conferences

The first warm-up is the reading and discussion of a poem in my group. It's how we begin every workshop—we immerse ourselves in strong diction, imagery, and themes, and we take away lessons about the qualities of effective writing. While I draw much poetry from my teaching anthology, *Naming the World*, this poem is by Josie, a member of the class.

In reading minilessons I had been teaching about the poetry and the impact of William Carlos Williams, whose mantra, "Say it—no ideas but in things," are words we live by in writing workshop. Concrete specifics bring a piece of writing to life. More importantly, observing the details of the world brings life to the imagination of a writer.

In the warm-up I ask kids to notice how Josie grounded the poem, which is included on the *Systems* DVD, in an observed experience and then brought to it her vision as a poet. At the end of the discussion, students add this technique to the section in their writing-reading handbooks where they record approaches they might try, gleaned from the poems we read together.

Helene's warm-up to writing workshop is an activity she calls *making words*. Her children practice listening to the sounds in words by manipulating letter strips in pocket holders. This helps prepare them to listen for sounds in the words they'll write, using invented spelling, during their independent writing time.

Jill brings a piece of her own writing to the minilesson. In this instance, she wrote a bad poem on purpose. Although she doesn't tell them this, its failings are those she observed in her kids' poems—first-person experiences without a first-person presence or an actor, lots of present participles (Jill calls them *–ing words*), and no personal reflection, all of which lead to a poem without theme or resonance.

None of us uses unsuccessful student writing to demonstrate what not to do—it's insensitive. But Jill has read tons of unfocused student drafts. It doesn't take her much time or

effort to compose an over-the-top bad version. After
she invites kids to describe what's wrong with her
poem, she asks what they would do to improve it. A
lesson like this gives students a fresh perspective when
reading their own drafts, along with strategies for
improving them.

In the first of four writing conferences that follow,
you'll see Fiona, a first grader, talk with Ted about the ideas she developed for a fairy tale
by depicting them in her sketchbook, and how Ted pushes her to expand from graphics to
language. In my conference with seventh-grader Natalie about her review of a television
program, I show her how to compose a conclusion that echoes the lead and fulfills its
promise. In her meeting with Jacob, Jill prompts him to generate and capture sensory
diction for a poem.

Glenn meets with fifth-grader Teddy in an editing conference. The day before, Teddy had
completed an editing checksheet, edited his memoir accordingly, and submitted it to Glenn to
copyedit. Now Glenn teaches him about a couple of the conventional errors he corrected the
night before, in this case about punctuating conversation. Teddy records the new conventions
on his individual proofreading list, to take responsibility for in future writing that includes dialogue. I've included on the *Systems* DVD two student proofreading lists, as well as an editing
checksheet, to exemplify the process that leads to individualized instruction in the meaningful
context of a student's own work.

Notice that in every case, teachers move—we go to our students. We control the length
of conferences and keep them short so that we may meet with many writers. We read
their drafts, rather than listening to them, because this is more efficient and because we're
responding, first, as readers. And because we are long-experienced readers of writing,
including student drafts, we have no compunctions about tapping that experience to offer
advice and suggestions.

Develop Your Own Writing Workshop

- Do what it takes to make writing inviting, meaningful, and worthwhile. This means freedom of choice, time to write, and encouragement and information along the way. Acknowledge that it's engaged practice that makes writers, and carve out time at least three days a week for students to write—preferably four or five.

- Begin to develop a repertoire of authentic genres to teach your students—developmentally appropriate versions of writing you can find in the real worlds of literature, journalism, and academia. Consult resources to plan minilessons that help children notice the features of a genre, develop topics for it, draft it, craft it, and revise and edit it.

- Create opportunities for students to raise their voices and go public as writers. CTL publishes *Acorns*, a non-juried, K–8 literary journal, two or three times a year and sends one home to every household. Our weekly newsletter features poems by students. Individual classroom teachers create cut-and-paste anthologies of students' writing at the end of a genre study and schedule a reading and celebration. And the teachers of children in grades K–2 publish individual booklets of their stories and reports.

- Remember that the teacher's main role in writing workshop is to talk with writers. Meet with individuals, engage in quiet conversations about what they're trying to do, and give them advice and information. Respond as a long-experienced reader, one who recognizes and wants clarity, logic, specifics, and grace. Offer suggestions that will move a writer and the writing forward. In minilessons to the group, demonstrate or explain workshop procedures, genres and their features, techniques of craft, topic generation and selection, and conventions of usage, format, and spelling. Institute writing handbooks in grades 3–8: spiral-bound class notebooks in which students record or insert minilesson information to refer to throughout a year of writing workshop.

Tap Resources About Writing Workshop

Teachers of grades 3–8 will find helpful information about writing workshop and minilessons in my books *In the Middle* and *Lessons That Change Writers*, as well as the demonstration teaching in my DVD project *Writing in the Middle: Workshop Essentials* (all from Heinemann).

Other resources I recommend include *Write to Learn* by Donald Murray (Holt, Rinehart, and Winston), *Writing: Teachers and Children at Work* by Donald Graves (Heinemann), and a collection of Graves' essays edited by Tom Newkirk and Penny Kittle, *Children Want to Write* (Heinemann).

For primary-grade teachers, we love *Talking, Drawing, Writing: Lessons for Our Youngest Writers* by Martha Horn and Mary Ellen Giacobbe (Stenhouse) and *Making Believe on Paper: Fiction Writing with Young Children* by Ted DeMille (Heinemann).

On the *Systems* DVD you'll find:

- Sample Writing Record, Grade 3 (Nicco)
- Sample Writing Record, Grade 8 (Xander)
- Sample Proofreading List, Grade 3 (Zoe)
- Sample Proofreading List, Grade 8 (Claire)
- Sample Editing Checksheet, Grade 8 (Claire)
- Expectations for Writing Workshop, Grades 1–2
- Expectations for Writing Workshop, Grades 7–8
- Rules for Writing Workshop, Grades 7–8

Sample Writing Record, Grade 3 (Nicco)

Jill Cotta
Center for Teaching and Learning

Name___Nicco___3___

WRITING RECORD

TITLE	GENRE	DATE FINISHED
Maggie	Bio-poem	9-10
Sand Castles	Poem	9-13
Rain	Poem	9-20
Pumpkin	Poem	10-3
Loki	Poem	10-14
Sand Dollars	Poem	11-3
Fish	Poem	11-19
Acorn	Poem	11-30
Gingerbread	poem	12-7
Hot Chocolate	Poem	12-14
Frostbite	Memoir	1-16
Riddle poem	Riddle	2-1
Squirrel	Poem	2-8
thieving Paws	Haiku	2-11
old One	Riddle poem	2-28
Hoku	Memoir	3-16

Sample Proofreading List, Grade 3 (Zoe)

_____ Zoe _____ 'S PROOFREADING LIST

1. Circle every word I'm not 100% certain of, i.e., its spelling.

2. Place a period when a sentence ends: where my voice drops and stops.

3. Break lines in poetry after strong words, short phrases, & punctuation.

4. Capitalize the first ____ ___ ___ ___ Sentence.

5. When writing dialo[g] paragraph every tim[e] speaks.

6. Capitalize first, last ___ in a title.

7. Capitalize names o[f] ___

8. Use the (¶ symbol) paragraph on ___

Sample Editing Checksheet, Grade 8 (Claire)

Nancie Atwell
Center for Teaching and Learning

EDITING CHECKSHEET

TO BE PAPER CLIPPED TO THE TOP OF YOUR WRITING SUBMITTED FOR TEACHER EDITING

NAME Claire _____

TITLE OF PIECE Whose Body? or ~~Depends~~ Who You're Fighting For

DATE OF PIECE 5/1

CONVENTION	EDITED (✓)	TEACHER'S COMMENTS
Look at every word, circle those I'm not 100% sure of and look them up.	✓	Check for apostrophes on possessive nouns.
Obvious stuff and capitalize first, last, and all important words in a title	✓	
Adjectives before a noun: no comma between the final adj. and the noun	✓	
Beware of comma splices	✓	
Listen for - and fix - ineffective repetition	✓	
Keep a constant verb tense: all past or all present	✓	**WORDS TO ADD TO MY PERSONAL SPELLING LIST**
Beware of too-long paragraphs	✓	who's = who is / whose = belongs to a who
Shifts in time in narratives need to be signaled with transitional phrases	✓	
Indent new paragraphs	✓	liable = reconcile
Review and refer to the rules of indicating titles, if any.	✓	

Sample Proofreading List, Grade 8 (Claire)

Claire_____'s Proofreading List

1. Obvious stuff

2. Look at every word, circle those I'm not 100% sure of, and look them up.

3. Capitalize first, last, and all important words in a title.

4. Adjectives before nouns, no comma between the final adjective and the noun.

5. Beware of comma splices

6. Listen for — and fix — ineffec...

7. Keep a consistent verb te...

8. Beware of too-long paragra...

9. Avoid "you" unless "you" mea... for or to.

10. Shifts in time in narrativ... transitional phrases.

11. Indent new paragraphs, i.e...

12. Review and refer to the...

13. Check for apostrophes on...

14.

Sample Writing Record, Grade 8 (Xander)

Nancie Atwell
Center for Teaching and Learning

Pieces of Writing Finished by Xander_____ during 2012-13

#	TITLE	GENRE	DATE COMPLETED
1	"Bittersweet"	Poem	9-26
2	"Home"	Poem	10-2
3	"October"	Collection of Haiku	10-4
4	"Xander"	Bio-poem	10-15
5	"Where I'm From"	Poem	10-19
6	"Child Fears"	Collaborative Poem	10-20
7	"everyday"	Gift of Writing	11-4
8	"The Darkness"	Memoir	12-4
9	"Standardized"	Poem	12-4
10	"The Boy"	Gift of Writing	12-19
11	"Our Moment"	Gift of Writing	12-19
12	"Violence & Redemption: Afghanistan"	Book Review	1-18
13	"Loki"	Poem	1-22
14	"Our Sonnet"	Sonnet	2-2
15	"Now"	Poem	2-21
16	"Teens and Cell Phones: Needless or Necessary?"	Essay	3-16
17	"Tsunami Dreams"	Microfiction	4-5
18	"What the Wind Knows"	Microfiction	4-4
19	"A Connection with the Land"	Advocacy Journalism	5-1

(over→)

" BECAUSE WE WANT OUR STUDENTS TO LOVE MATHEMATICS, THE APPROACHES WE TAKE ARE MULTISOURCE AND INTERDISCIPLINARY, DESIGNED TO EXCITE STUDENTS AND CREATE COMPETENT, CONFIDENT MATHEMATICIANS. "

6

Math Workshop

Talk About It and Reflect

Consider these questions:

- What do you want your students to understand about mathematics? What do you want them to be good at as mathematicians when they leave your classroom?
- What's the balance in your math program among lessons, discussions, small group work, and independent efforts?
- What roles do vocabulary development and writing play?
- What opportunities do your students have to demonstrate or explore their interests as mathematicians?
- How do you show your interest in your students as mathematicians?

Read About Math Workshop

Should math instruction be concept-driven or computation-driven? A mathematician will tell you the answer is both—that skills and facts need to be automatic in order to ease engagement in higher conceptual thinking. We work hard at CTL on both fronts. Our kids get lots of practice with computation through such strategies as mental math, brush-ups, warm-ups, and, for students in grades 5–8, the IXL website, which they tackle as homework. One goal is for students to be able to rely on the automaticity of their computational skills as they attempt to solve higher-order problems.

Another is for students to be able to *think* as mathematicians, and the best tool we know for concept formulation is vocabulary. There's a tremendous amount of discussion in our math workshops, as well as frequent opportunities for students to write as mathematicians in journals, logs, and self-assessments. As they write their way through math problems and analyze their progress, they engage in the highest-quality thinking of all.

Math at CTL emphasizes activities and lessons that help students understand the value of mathematics, master number facts, reason and communicate mathematically, feel confident in their math abilities, understand and use the vocabulary of mathematicians, and become versatile problem solvers. Teachers show students how to collaborate, look for more than one way to answer a question, and work through temporary confusions. We set a tone and develop activities that push kids to go beyond rote learning. Because we want our students to love mathematics, the approaches we take are multisource and interdisciplinary, designed to excite students and create competent, confident mathematicians.

In kindergarten, Helene draws on Everyday Math, the geometry section of the Investigations program, and other supplementary materials. Ted's and Jill's grades 1–4 curriculum is based on Investigations and supplemented with Math Their Way, Math Solutions, and NCTM resources and materials. In grades 5–6, Glenn's students experience two units from Investigations; the remainder of their program consists of the Connected Mathematics Project, which allows kids to recreate the process of discovery that led to the development of particular math concepts and, along the way, learn the concepts in deep, meaningful ways. CMP—supplemented by rich activities that draw on art, science, literature, and history—is the heart of Katie Rittershaus' program in grades 7–8.

Teachers establish the focus of each day's math workshop in the minilesson, which is always preceded by a warm-up—a routine or exercise that focuses children's attention and prepares them to think mathematically. In K–2, these include all kinds of counting, the solution of a few addition and subtraction problems, numeral formation and the reading of numbers, easy mental-math addition strings (zeros, ones, and twos), and word problems based on the work the children are focusing on in science and history. Jill's third and fourth graders sit in a circle and pass a Koosh ball as she assigns them a mental-math exercise, for example, performing two-digit addition and subtraction with regrouping, counting by multiples of three through twelve, or supplying multiplication and division facts. In fifth and sixth grades, Glenn starts each math workshop with the problems of the day: three or four straightforward mental or paper computations as a review of previous units of study.

In grades 7–8, Katie's math workshop begins with a brush-up: a five- to ten-minute computational checkup composed of questions about the basic binary operation of integers. These sets of problems might also include questions about the meaning of a math term, such as *algorithm*, *prime factorization*, and *least common multiple*, or the significance of a math symbol. Here's a typical 7–8 brushup.

1. $\dfrac{3\frac{1}{2}}{\frac{4}{5}}$ 2. $.56 \times 1.73$ 3. $13.001 - .06595$

4. $.56/9688$ 5. $17\frac{1}{4} - \frac{4}{9}$

Bonus: Write the base$_2$ number 1011 in base$_{10}$.

Beginning a class with a computational brushup accomplishes two things: it helps students transition from recess or history class to the mind-set of math workshop, and it requires them to apply skills on a daily basis and improve their accuracy, understanding, and speed. Katie's brushup is followed by a mental-math exercise: a l-o-n-g number sentence read aloud to the class. As the year progresses, seventh and eighth graders volunteer to design brushup and mental-math challenges for their group.

Math minilessons address three areas. *Procedural* lessons teach kids how to be productive in the math workshop; these focus on such issues as organization of binders or folders, where manipulatives are stored, and how to use calculators. *Conventions* lessons introduce strategies, vocabulary, and basic operations. The remaining minilessons introduce key *concepts*, which CTL teachers have grouped under five strands: number and operations, measurement, data analysis and probability, geometry, and algebra.

The minilesson sets the stage for individual or small-group work. After the teacher—or a student—introduces an activity or problem to further the class's understanding of a procedure, convention, or concept, students engage, and their teacher circulates among them.

Glenn assigns his fifth and sixth graders to math study teams. In September, he pairs two veterans with two students new to his class to create a small group that stays together for the first unit of math study. After that, as the units change, he assigns the groups randomly. Glenn's list of rules for math study teams, included on the Systems DVD, defines how the groups function—how kids work independently but also rely on team members for support and feedback as each student assesses his or her nightly homework, looking for problems that are either "stumpers" or "professors." A professor is a problem that a student feels confident about—it's one he or she can teach to the rest of the team. A stumper is a problem the student couldn't solve. Kids write two specific questions about their stumpers, bring these to their study team, and ask for help. This homework routine is a built-in reflection process that makes individual students accountable for clearing up misunderstandings and acquiring skills and strategies.

We know that students' command of academic vocabulary is integral to their success in every subject. Our math vocabulary efforts are informed by the insightful work of author and mathematician Miki Murray, who taught at CTL until her retirement. The grades 7–8 class focuses on vocabulary by writing daily math reflections (three minutes at most) at the end of each class; bi-weeklies, which are self-evaluations of the previous two weeks of math study; the unit investigation reflections that are included in the CMP program; word walls, which are self-defined, alphabetized lists of math vocabulary; and an overarching self-evaluation at the end of each trimester.

In kindergarten, students use simple math journals to demonstrate their understandings of concepts and vocabulary. At first Helene writes a term for them, and they depict its meaning by drawing an illustration, based on a relevant math activity. By mid-year, children create their own labels and captions for their illustrations of new math terminology.

At the start of each math concept study in grades 1–2, Ted introduces the relevant vocabulary. He defines the words in a minilesson, and then the children practice writing them on individual whiteboards. Afterward, students record the words in the vocabulary section of their math notebooks, and Ted expects and helps them to use the terms when talking and writing about math.

Jill's third and fourth graders create a math vocabulary lexicon in the spiral notebooks that serve as their math journals, organized under headings of the five math strands. They refer to the lexicon when explaining mathematical concepts, orally and in writing. Glenn's and Katie's math students create individual word walls, an invention of Miki Murray's, as a place for students to gather, define, exemplify, and review math vocabulary.

Glenn also devises study-group tests that consist of a few complex problems. After students work on these independently, they share their solutions with their teammates. Glenn audio-records the conversations to listen to later so that he can assess students' use of math vocabulary, their attention to the math ideas of peers, and their ability to articulate their own methods. Each student selects one teammate's solution as exemplary and writes a reflection about it. Finally, based on the conversation, they describe the modifications they would make to their own solutions.

Watch Warm-Ups and Minilessons

The warm-ups and brushups featured on the DVD show Ted, Jill, Glenn, and Katie bringing their students into math mode at the start of the workshop. As you watch their pre-workshop routines, notice how:

- Ted's students use whiteboards for computation practice.

- Jill's kids take pleasure in reviewing multiplication facts around the minilesson circle because the Koosh ball makes a game of it.

- Jill acknowledges the spread of abilities in her grades 3–4 group by providing computation practice at two levels of difficulty, plus an "extra" hard problem.

- Jill's students use computation notebooks and share their approaches and thinking as problem-solvers.

- Glenn's students enter class to find the P.O.D. (Problems of the Day) on the board and work to solve them while he circulates and checks their homework; then the children and Glenn unpack P.O.D. answers and strategies together.

- Glenn confers with each study team about the previous night's homework assignment and how they have helped teammates solve any stumpers.

- Glenn's minilesson on decimal-based fractions for multiplication is in response to a problem he observed in student work. His kids both participate in the lesson and record it in their math notebooks.

- Katie's students use math vocabulary to talk their way through their demonstrations of the strategies they used to solve the brush-up equations, plus how Katie asks for alternative strategies.

- Josie, a seventh grader, volunteered to design and conduct the mental math practice in her group.

- Katie's vocabulary loop game pushes her students, hard, to master the language and concepts of mathematicians.

Develop Your Own Math Workshop

- Do whatever it takes to make mathematics inviting, joyful, and meaningful. This means access to multivalent curricula that incorporate manipulatives and tools, authentic problems, skills practice, and opportunities for discussion, reflection, and writing, with an emphasis on the connections among mathematics and other disciplines. Acknowledge that it's engaged practice that creates mathematicians. Ensure that students have math four or five days a week.

- Build a classroom environment that immerses students in mathematics. This includes calendars, manipulatives, games and toys, literature, tools, inspiring quotations and other posters, and any resource that highlights the integral role of mathematics in the modern world. Plan lessons that encourage students to explore concepts, problem-solve, and apply their skills. Incorporate real-life mathematics as often as possible through films, books, and articles from newspapers and magazines. Continuously assess methods, and make adaptations as research reveals new implications for the classroom.

- Create opportunities for students to use mathematics throughout the school day. One way CTL does this is through our monthly estimation jar: students are shown an extrapolation jar filled with an identified number of an item and encouraged to use it as a reference. Their estimates are collected, sorted, and graphed, and the results are announced at morning meeting, where the winner explains his or her method. Other opportunities include kindergarten cooking and measuring; calendar work; read-alouds of children's literature about mathematics; card games, chess, and checkers at recess; surveys and other data collection and analysis used by students to inform persuasive essays; and Math Counts, an afternoon math program for students in grades 6–8.

- Remember that the teacher's main role is to talk with mathematicians. Meet with individuals or small groups and engage in conversations about their approaches and strategies. Offer support when it's needed. Provide thoughtful responses to written assignments, and encourage improvement in students' understandings *and* in their articulation of what they understand. At the start of each class, engage students as mathematicians and review operations through brushups, mental math, and other forms of computational practice. In minilessons, demonstrate or explain workshop procedures, mental math, computation strategies, conventions, problems and processes from the five strands, the calendar in K–2, math biography presentations in 7–8, and, across the grades, mathematical vocabulary.

- Encourage students to become teachers—to share strategies at the board or in small groups. Promote the development of individual students' special interests in math by providing them with additional resources and extra challenges, and meet with them to discuss this work. Above all, be enthusiastic about math, and invite and expect kids to be excited, too.

Tap Resources About Math Workshop

The *Systems* DVD provides a sampling of guidelines and student work that illustrate math workshops:

- Expectations for Math Workshop, Grades 3–4
- Rules for Math Study Teams, Grades 5–6
- Guidelines for Math Journals and Binders, Grades 7–8
- Sample Daily Math Reflections, Grade 7 (Sophia)
- Sample Biweekly Math Self-Evaluation, Grade 7 (Amelia)
- Sample Kindergarten Math Journal Entry

CTL teachers are fans of the work of our former colleague, Miki Murray. Her books *Teaching Mathematics Vocabulary in Context: Windows, Doors, and Secret Passageways* and *The Differentiated Math Classroom: A Guide for Teachers, K–8*, both published by Heinemann, have helped shape our math instruction. We think that *Putting the Practices into Action* by Susan O'Connell and John SanGiovanni (Heinemann) is a great new resource for K–8 teachers.

We've also benefited from NCTM publications and the work of Marilyn Burns, especially her *About Teaching Mathematics: A K–8 Resource, Second Edition* (Math Solutions Publications). Each of the teachers owns, and all the seventh and eighth graders are required to purchase, *The Mathematics Dictionary and Handbook* (Nichols Schwartz).

Sample Daily Math Reflections, Grade 7 (Sophia)

SAMPLE DAILY MATH REFLECTIONS - Grade 7

DMR   10/31

Today in class I reviewed how
to find mean, median, & mode. Ex.:
mode= greatest # of 1 piece of data
mean= add all the data, then ÷ by the
# of data
median= if you put all the data in
order of value, which number/
amount would be in the middle

1/17 DMR

Today in class I learned to maintain equality.
I could add, subtract, multiply, or divide both sides of
the equality by the same number. These are called the
properties of equality, which is how I get/find X
in an equation.

DMR   2/8

Today in class I learn
digit in the standard form
high power. Ex.: 4.8G7

4's repeating 1 digits
9G7÷2=483 r1
The ones digit= 4

2/15   DMR

Today in class I learned
factor: 12÷y1. It's the san
the growth rate for an

x	y
0	400
1	200
2	100
3	50
4	25
5	12.6

Sample Biweekly Math Self-Evaluation, Grade 7 (Amelia)

Miki Murray
Adapted with permission by Katie Rittershaus
Center for Teaching and Learning

Biweekly Mathematics Self-Evaluation
Grades 7 and 8

Name: Amelia   Dates Covered: 3/31

1. Summarize the mathematics concepts we have studied during the above time period.
We have worked with writing equivalent expressions And
how to use a diagram to write an expression/equation.
Also how to tell what part of an expression represents
the part of a diagram you are able to see.

2. Look over the class work you have completed and the notes you have taken. Please
describe your journal work. Include beginnings, mini-lessons, and daily math reflections.
Tell how complete you have been in recording information or what you feel you need to do
to be more complete. Give examples when necessary.
I have been forgetting to do DMRs, but my class work is
thorough & neat. Some of the questions I have needed help from
classmates eg. problem 1.4 E, but other than that I
understand every concept.

3. From the material we've covered, elaborate on one concept that represents your most
significant understanding. Give evidence of the level of your understanding. What
questions would you like answered and what help do you need?
The Distributive Property I understand very much because
of using it in the Algebra book. Those lessons helped
me a lot in this Investigation. ⟶

4. Look over the homework you have done. Does it include all assignments? If not,
explain why. Point out parts that were challenging, difficult to understand, or difficult to
complete. Vocabulary entries are part of your weekly homework assignments. Look over
your vocabulary for neatness and completeness. Summarize all these items.
The only time my work wasn't complete was when I forgot
to do A.C.E #I, #58. Other than that it is complete. My
WORD WALL is neat & complete & everything is explained
to my fullest.

5. Think about your effort, behavior, and class participation in mathematics over the last
two weeks. How cooperative, responsible, and supportive have you been? What
improvements could you make?
It participated a lot compared to before. Now all I
need to do it participate even more.

Rules for Math Study Teams, Grades 5–6

(Glenn Powers)

- Math is tough for some, easier for others. We will honor and respect all questions, ideas, attempts at solutions, and ways of solving problems. Don't rush ahead in your work: your study team is not done until everyone is done.

- Use some form of a problem-solving strategy for *every* problem you solve: draw a diagram, find key words, organize your data, use charts or tables, find patterns, guess and check, make it simpler, break it into smaller parts, find friendly numbers, estimate, and so on.

- Write down all your thoughts on the page to show how deeply you understand something and to track your process. Show all your work. Put everything down on paper, even when using a calculator. Cross out work with one line; never erase.

- Date and label each assignment and organize your work on the page in a way that's easy to follow and clearly understandable.

- Start by working independently. Attempt each problem. You are responsible for your own understandings. The goal here is for you to understand how to solve problems independently; just getting answers from a teammate won't help you achieve it.

- Ask your study teammates first, before asking me. Ask specific questions that pinpoint your confusion.

- You **must** help teammates who ask you a question. Remember that at some point you'll need

Sample Kindergarten Math Journal Entry (Aidan)

© 2014 by Nancie Atwell from *Systems to Transform Your Classroom and School*. Portsmouth, NH: Heinemann.

Expectations for Math Workshop, Grades 3–4

(Jill Cotta)

- Know and understand facts and concepts under five math strands: number and operations, measurement, data analysis and probability, geometry, and algebra.
- Learn the purpose of mathematical concepts by participating in many different experiences—understand how they help you solve problems in everyday life.
- Use math facts and concepts you have learned to solve problems in all parts of your life.
- Be an active problem solver: analyze, predict, make decisions, and evaluate your solutions and mathematical thinking.
- Learn the vocabulary of mathematics throughout the math strands, and use math language orally and in writing.
- Participate in whole-group and small-group math activities.
- During small group mathematical tasks:
    - listen to others' ideas about procedures and solutions
    - be willing to help any group member who asks
    - seek help from group members
    - make sure that everyone has an equal chance to speak and contribute to some part of the solution
- Explain your mathematical thinking and ideas both orally and in writing.
- Use your math journal to write about mathematical ideas, solve problems, explain how you solved a problem, gather and organize data, record vocabulary, and set goals.
- Try some of the math extension activities for small group and individuals.
- Take care of CTL's math manipulatives and tools. Keep manipulatives sorted and in good condition. Return math tools to their appropriate places.
- Work hard, challenge yourself, master multiplication and division facts, try new problem-solving strategies, and become an independent mathematical thinker and problem solver, as well as a member of a community of mathematicians.

Guidelines for Math Journals and Binders, Grades 7–8

(Katie Rittershaus, adapted with permission from Miki Murray)

Your graphing calculator should be kept in the front of your binder in the zippered nylon case, followed by your Connected Mathematics Project book. Your homework log sheets should be the first pages in your binder, before the divided sections. Every assignment is to be listed on the log as to when it was given to you and when it's due. There's an additional space provided for comments. In this column, you may note if the assignment was a *review*, a *favorite*, or a *challenge*. These comments may help you later in the trimester, during self-evaluation when you're assessing favorite or challenging assignments. The homework log is your personal record; a portion of it will be included in your portfolio.

Your **Journal** is the first divided section in your binder. You'll use it for recording on a daily basis. It should include the following:

- All work you do on in-class problems: words, charts, pictures, diagrams, or anything else to show your thinking.
- Notes you take during minilessons or conversations. Write anything that will help you remember what you were thinking, so that you can refer back to it for help.
- Your daily *mathematical reflections*: a summary of the math concepts you encountered during class, including new understandings, questions about the topic, and connections to other areas of math or other subjects.

Homework is the next divided section. This is where in-process and completed assignments are kept, so you'll always know where your homework is. After we go over it in class and/or it's checked by me, you'll file it in your *returns* section (see below).

Forms and Guides follow the homework section. This is where you'll store my expectations handout, guidelines, rubrics, and so forth, throughout the year.

The **Returns** section is next. You'll keep papers here until the completion of a unit; then they'll go into your archives. This section stores returned homework, quizzes, brush-ups, and so on.

Math Vocabulary is the last section in your binder. You'll set aside three spaces for each math term you enter: a definition, an illustration, and examples. The definitions may change over time as your understanding develops and expands, so be sure to leave extra room. Your **Word Wall** will be kept at the end of the vocabulary section. You'll use it to index the vocabulary and keep track of your vocabulary development.

Your journal, homework, and vocabulary will be the basis for your **Biweekly Self-Evaluation**. On alternate weeks, I'll collect your journal pages to evaluate and respond to.

© 2014 by Nancie Atwell from *Systems to Transform Your Classroom and School*. Portsmouth, NH: Heinemann.

"Even in a school like ours, with a unified curriculum and philosophy, there must be room for teachers to be expressive. Methods are how good teachers express themselves."

7

Innovations

Talk About It and Reflect

- Consider a recent time you tried something new in your classroom, and describe what happened.
- How does your school culture support teachers who are trying or developing new instructional approaches?
- What opportunities do teachers at your school have to develop and share ideas, discuss successes and struggles, and reflect together on your practice?

Read About CTL Innovations

There are so many commonalities among our classes at CTL that I sometimes think a kindergartner could wander into my 7–8 writing workshop, settle into the minilesson circle, and then move off at independent writing time and start drafting away. Obviously, there are differences. Although we conform to a workshop model in writing, reading, and math, within and across the grades teachers respond to who our students are and what they need by developing methods that support and enrich the workshop model.

Helene's and Ted's K–2 writers keep sketchbooks, in which they learn from their teachers how to draw, develop ideas for writing topics, tell stories, and record the world around them. Older writers have access to clipboards and often head outside to gather sensory data. My students begin every writing workshop by reading and unpacking a poem together. Glenn asks writers to use a revision sticker system—to list on blank labels the particular revision techniques they attempted in a given piece of writing, attach them to the draft, and, in the process, make conscious and purposeful use of his minilessons about craft. Jill's third and fourth graders keep spelling notebooks. Ted uses song writing to help his students learn information and concepts. The workshop model is generous and flexible.

To deny teachers opportunities to innovate—to respond to who their children are and what they need—is a sure-fire way to kill a sense of professionalism. There's a kind of authoring that good teachers do, a writing in air that involves observing students, inventing, planning, experimenting, and assessing. At the same time that CTL is a K–8 school with models and principles that cut across grades, we acknowledge that teaching is and must be a generative profession.

I worry that in the current political climate, bright young people who are creative thinkers may not be as drawn to teaching, because scripted and mandated programs undercut innovation. This is something teachers need to fight for: the right to be responsive to our students and think creatively about our methods. There's a world of difference between following instructions as a technician and deliberating, generating, and acting as a professional. Even in a school like ours, with a unified curriculum and philosophy, there must be room for teachers to be expressive. Methods are how good teachers express themselves.

And methods are the *interesting* part of education. I confess I don't understand teachers who leave the classroom for administrative positions. There's nothing more satisfying or powerful than figuring out how to teach and be with children. It's easy to be script-bound. It's hard to innovate, but the challenge of it is what invites intellectually ambitious people into the profession and, along with opportunities for collaboration and mentorship, keeps them here.

So while there is a common talk and walk at CTL, faculty members are urged to experiment, with the aim of deeper engagement and enhanced learning. It's an interesting balance; in the process, we get to learn from one another. The drawing lessons that Helene began in kindergarten evolved into the work Ted's students do with sketchbooks, just as Helene's students' poetry binders were so successful that students in grades 1–4 now collect binders of poems, too. An individualized approach to spelling instruction migrated down from my group to Jill's and Glenn's, along with the correspondences I initiated with kids about books. CTL students benefit from the innovations of their own teacher, along with those of the entire faculty.

I'll focus on a handful of innovations that panned out in remarkable ways, methods that transformed children and gratified their teacher-authors. The first is Helene's use of poetry to teach reading to kindergartners.

Poetry Invites and Teaches Readers

Helene's kindergarten literacy program was already rich. It consisted of a daily reading workshop, guided and choral reading of each day's class message, read-alouds, author and illustrator studies, shared reading of big books, a drawing and writing workshop, emphasis on the phonetics of invented spelling, attention to the spelling of high-frequency words, and kindergartners' tutelage by fourth-grade reading buddies. Incorporating poetry into her mix of methods has had the single most powerful impact on her students' growth as readers.

Helene devotes planning time each week to skimming collections of contemporary verse written for children and looking for keepers—poems she loves and predicts her kindergartners will fall in love with, too. The small, fresh stories and images she selects become the heart of her word work. She copies a poem on an oak tag chart in her large, careful printing, attaches it with rings to a chart stand, and uses its language and patterns to determine the focus of her next literacy lesson.

When the kindergartners gather around the chart stand each morning, seated on braided mats, Helene invites them to enter a world of wonderful words—sensory and evocative diction, language compressed to its essence, and ideas, feelings, experiences, and themes that ring true for five- and six-year-olds. Children love the poems for their sounds, meanings, and stories. Their teacher's lessons enable the kindergartners to make the wonderful words their own.

Helene weaves in a curriculum of reading and writing strategies: voice-print matching, letter identification, sight words, predictions based on semantics and syntax, sounding out, attention to punctuation, identification of known words inside unfamiliar ones, phonograms, suffixes, consonant digraphs, compound words, and diction choices that she and the kids call "rich words."

Helene introduces two poems each week. She makes her choices based on the level of readability for her kids at that juncture in the school year, what's interesting to her students, and seasonal events. In addition to copying the words onto a chart, she also makes typed photocopies of the poem. She inserts these in plastic sleeves and clips the sleeved poems into three-ring poetry binders, one for each child. On Fridays, the kindergartners review the two new poems, along with old favorites from their binders. Later that afternoon, they read the new poems to their fourth-grade reading buddies. Over the weekend, they take their binders home, illustrate the new poems, practice reading them to their parents, and revisit old favorites.

A Group of Kindergartners with Their Poetry Binders

The result is a double blessing. Children learn to read with more exuberance than Helene has witnessed in a long career of teaching kindergarten, and they achieve fluency and independence sooner in the school year than ever before. The rhythms, patterns, repetitions and cadence, imagery, diction, and brevity of contemporary poems for children, along with the meaningful stories they tell, engage kindergartners and invite expression and comprehension. But the children also carry away in their hearts and minds a repertoire of beloved poems to savor in years to come, as they relate the new experiences of their lives to the stories, images, and language they voiced, internalized, and loved in kindergarten.

Kindergarten and Fourth-Grade Reading Buddies

Helene has chosen not to go it alone as a teacher of reading. In addition to asking parents to support nightly reading and providing them with guidance about how to help their children learn to read, she commandeers Jill's fourth graders.

Helene and Jill sit down together in the first days of school, contemplate their class lists, and pair each incoming kindergartner with a fourth grader. These twosomes are a highlight of a child's career at CTL—the K–4 relationships resonate for years to come. Fourth graders shepherd their buddies through the ropes of our school: morning meetings, field trips, portfolio preparation, and science and history collaborations. On Fridays, they teach the kindergartners how to read.

Our protocol for training students to become reading tutors draws on the work of Marie Clay. Each Thursday afternoon, while her own class is in art, Helene meets with the fourth graders for five minutes during their reading workshop time. Based on where her students are as readers, she selects either a new method to introduce to the fourth graders or techniques for them to reinforce—for example, echo reading, finger reading, or rewinding. Helene's curriculum for the yearlong reading buddies program is included on the *Systems* DVD.

On Friday afternoons, the little ones crawl onto the big ones' laps, settle, and for half an hour practice their reading routine. The results are powerful. The kindergartners receive expert assistance from readers who were in their shoes recently enough that they can recall their own passage into literacy, and the fourth graders get to do the real work—and feel the real satisfaction—of helping someone they love learn how to read.

Whiteboards Across the Curriculum

Individual dry-erase boards have become an essential tool in Ted's teaching across the curriculum. Each of his first and second graders writes and draws on a 9" × 12" whiteboard throughout the school day, in every subject.

During minilessons, first and second graders record vocabulary in math, science, and history on their whiteboards, and then capture the words permanently in notebooks in each subject so they may tap them later in their writing across the curriculum. In math, they record warm-ups and brushups, practice forming numerals and drawing geometric shapes, collect data, estimate, and engage in number sequence, place value, and computation activities.

Children practice the formation of upper- and lower-case letters on their whiteboards. They engage in word work, writing, for example, common consonant combinations (*ch, wh, str*) or vowel chunks (*-ake, -ain, -eat*). They learn the fundamentals of drawing from step-by-step demonstrations Ted provides on a large whiteboard of his own, and they use their drawings to help them generate writing ideas and details for poems, stories, reports, and memoirs.

Sophia's Whiteboard Plans for a Fairy Tale

Ted shows his students techniques for planning pieces of writing on whiteboards. They draw settings, main characters, and plot points—the beginnings, middles, and ends of stories. They draw the "nugget" of a memoir and sketch its before, its after, and their reflections about both. When his kids write nonfiction, Ted demonstrates how to divide a whiteboard into fields and fill each with a different kind of information, which children then incorporate into drafts of brochures, booklets, and posters.

The whiteboards are a hit. They're fun to use and also forgiving—mistakes can be wiped away with ease, and revisions are quick to make, too. The children appreciate that they're saving paper, with the understanding that a significant image can be photocopied or photographed before it's erased. Ted appreciates the reliability and flexibility of dry-erase boards: he doesn't have to worry about technology failing him during a minilesson demonstration, and he can teach a whole class, guide a small group, or establish an ad hoc learning center.

Best of all, from Ted's perspective, is that he can engage and assess every child. As the class gathers on the carpet at his feet, he knows by looking around the circle who's grasping a concept and who needs redirection or reteaching—the numbers, letters, words, and images on their whiteboards show him.

I know that tech-savvy folks are reading this and thinking that Ted's lessons could just as well be accomplished with iPads and Smart Boards. We do use technology at CTL. Children in grades 4–8 compose on laptops, and older students conduct Internet research throughout their school day. But teachers recognize that high tech doesn't automatically equal high quality or resonant learning. A student's colorful, detailed, hand-drawn poster of the life cycle of a bat or a cross section of a World War I trench has immense value as an artifact, a learning experience, and a permanent presentation of a child's knowledge. It's also easy to display, portable, and often beautiful.

Something unique and creative happens when Ted picks up his dry-erase marker, his kids take hold of theirs, and black-line images flow from their hearts and brains, through their fingertips, and onto the canvases of their whiteboards.

Reader's Roundtable

In his grades 5–6 reading workshop, Glenn schedules a reader's roundtable every Wednesday—a text-based, whole-class, student-led discussion about a specific literary topic, which kids prepare for beforehand, take notes on during, and reflect on afterward.

These are not literature circles. In general, none of the kids is reading and discussing the same title, because they've made their book selections based on their individual tastes and abilities. Rather, each reader addresses the same literary question, posed by Glenn, about his or her book of choice. For example, Glenn has asked them to consider: "Did your author make a movie of the story? If so, when and how?" "What was the problem or conflict in your book? What makes a fictional problem compelling?" "What narrative voice did your author choose? What are some of the reasons an author chooses one perspective over another?" "What makes a great main character?" "How do you identify the genre of a book? What are some defining features of different genres?"

The day before a reader's roundtable, Glenn introduces the question of the week and gives kids guidance about how to prepare for it. Each student is required to come to the roundtable discussion with an index card on which he or she has copied evidence paragraphs from two books. They use the title they're currently reading and a second they've finished as sources to back up their opinions about the assigned topic. The 30–50 minute roundtable discussion takes place the next day. The day after that there's a recap of about ten minutes, as the reading workshop minilesson.

Glenn's roundtable opens up reading workshop to literary discussions that reward focus, citation, and engaged, critical reading. When I sit in with his class on a roundtable day, I'm in awe. His fifth and sixth graders, with little input from Glenn, can talk about books at a grad-school level, their contributions are that serious, thoughtful, and text based. Choice doesn't undercut rigor, especially when a teacher shows kids how to analyze and describe literature as critics do. The *Systems* DVD includes Glenn's guidelines for "What Makes a Good Discussion in a Reader's Roundtable."

Letter-Essays About Literature

Letters about literature are another reading workshop innovation. In the 1980s, I was intrigued by written dialogues that Leslee Reed, a sixth-grade teacher, exchanged with her class—letters about students' lives, written back and forth in bound journals. My interest was piqued because I knew my students had more to say about their books than time allowed in my daily check-ins in reading workshop, and because I'd learned by then what a rich mode for thinking writing could be. I wondered where written-down conversations about books might lead my students as critics. So I gave each of them a notebook with a letter inside from me, inviting them to write back about their reading. Thirty years later, I'm still corresponding with my students about books and still experimenting with the method, in search of the most manageable and productive version.

One early revision resulted from the paper load. I had seventy-five students in the 1980s, and answering a letter a week from each of them proved exhilarating but exhausting. Another refinement grew from the uneven quality of the letters. The best ones were written after a student had finished a book. These responses were longer and more thoughtful, referred with more specificity to the text and the author's choices, delved more into theme, and, in general, functioned more as literary—albeit still informal—criticism.

I went back to the drawing board again and again. Literary correspondence in my reading workshop today takes the form of letter-essays that students write to me or a classmate every three weeks about a title they have finished reading. While still conversational in tone, letter-essays have proved more demanding, more forgiving, and more valuable to my students than the chat of weekly literary correspondence.

Letter-essays are required to fill at least three pages of a marble notebook. By considering one book at length, students go deep. By looking back and choosing *the one* book of the past three weeks they wish to criticize, they engage as critics. Because writing about their thinking makes anyone think better, my students are smarter than ever about literature—about recognizing an author's techniques, purposes, and themes. And because their high school and college English teachers will ask them to write critical responses in which they develop arguments based on textual evidence, the letter-essays provide a strong bridge into what comes next for middle schoolers as students of literature. The *Systems* DVD includes the September letter I write to each of them, spelling out rationales and requirements, along with an example of an exchange between two students.

My students' letter-essays are interesting to read and easier for me to reply to than weekly correspondence, because there's more literary meat to them. When I write back, I affirm their insights or challenge them, offer my opinions, make suggestions and recommendations, float theories, provide information, compliment their ideas and observations, and, as necessary, give pointers for the next letter-essay.

Mathematician Biographies

CTL students know about Katie Rittershaus' mathematician biography project before they enter seventh grade, so it's not far into the school year before they begin to ask, "When are we going to be matched to a mathematician?" As younger students, they observed the 7–8 class setting out a ton of food in preparation for the presentations. It's a party, and it happens three times a year.

The math bio project launches every year on or near September 19, the day that mathematician Andrew Wiles solved Fermat's Last Theorem. While Katie's classes usually start with a computational brushup and a mental-math exercise, that day, when they enter the room, her students discover A&W® root beer floats, in honor of Andrew Wiles. Wiles is the ideal role model for teaching students to expect difficulty and value perseverance, because the story of his solution of Fermat's Last Theorem illustrates the challenges and satisfactions students can anticipate when they study math. Katie presents a beguiling version of Wiles' biography to the group—and also tells the stories of the mathematicians who struggled with the theorem before him and without whose contributions his success wouldn't have been possible. Her demonstration provides a model for how kids should research and bring to life the story of their own mathematicians.

Katie makes the matches between particular students and mathematicians based on the results of a quirky, multiple-choice "personality test." She asks students to identify first names from a list from different cultures that strike their fancy, and also the time periods, countries, and academic subjects that most intrigue them. She queries them about how they would describe their own personalities, why math is important in their lives, their plans for the future, favorite branches of higher mathematics, and cities they'd like to visit or learn about someday. Students' answers give her insights about how their interests align with the lives, work, eras, and countries of origin of the mathematicians on her master list of the greats.

She selects the mathematicians that kids study to complement the concepts she covers in the Connected Mathematics Project curriculum, which means that the class will hear a student's presentation about Pythagoras in the same trimester as Katie teaches the CMP text *Looking for Pythagoras.* The presentations, which also include the life story and character of each mathematician, focus on his or her greatest achievements. They expose students to some of the seminal, most fascinating concepts in the history of math, their development, and their application.

Katie's list of mathematicians is partially derived from volumes 1 and 2 of the Reimers' *Mathematicians Are People, Too* (Dale Seymour), which include many of the greats—Hypatia, Descartes, and Fibonacci, among others. While these books are a great place to begin to build a list, to emphasize the flexibility and universality of mathematics, Katie also

includes famous physicists, architects, artists, code breakers, and other influential members of mathematically inclined disciplines, such as Arakawa and Gins, Fritz Zwicky and Walter Baade, and Alan Turing. You'll find seventh-grader Xander's biography of "Many Worlds" theorist Hugh Everett on the *Systems* DVD.

The mathematician biography project has met with extraordinary success with our students. They enjoy preparing their presentations and listening to others', and they routinely identify it in math self-evaluations as one of their favorite activities of the year. Most importantly, they get to vicariously experience the lives, struggles, and triumphs of men and women who gave their all to the purposes, meanings, and mysteries of math.

Amelia and Pythagoras, Her Mathematician Match

A Spiral Curriculum in Science and History

It was exciting for us in the early days of CTL to contemplate the nature and shape of a brand-new content-area curriculum. The workshop model was a given in our teaching of writing, reading, and math. Science and social studies were wide open. We could begin from scratch to define the concepts, knowledge, and skills we believed to be essential outcomes for our students. And we could determine how deep we wanted children to go, as researchers and reporters of science and social studies topics, instead of settling for coverage.

First, we decided to replace social studies with history—to introduce children to the individuals, events, causes, decisions, and consequences that led to who they are and how and where they live. Next, we determined to bring science to life for children, with rich readings as well as experiments, observations, data collection and analysis, construction and design projects, field trips, quests, guest experts, and explorations in the arts. Finally, we teachers wanted to be able to collaborate as planners of history and science—to put our heads together, generate deep and engaging curricula, and create occasions across a school year for the children at our school to work and learn in collaboration.

The result is a five-year spiral curriculum. In each year of the cycle, the topics we study in science and history, K–8, revolve around two themes. Concepts addressed during students' early years at CTL are revisited when they're older and ready for review, subtleties, and greater depth. Our paired emphases in science and history are *systems* (weather, human biology, and astronomy) and *Western civilization* (Egypt, Greece, Rome, medieval Europe, and the Renaissance); *water* and *making a nation*; *geology-paleontology* and *19th century America*; *woods and wildlife* and *immigration and the first half of the 20th century*; and *energy and invention* and *who we are today*.

Students engage as researchers of the paired concepts and learn in-depth and collaboratively about the natural and physical worlds and how history is shaped. Along the way, they encounter a chronology of American history, an introduction to Western culture, and a balance of natural and physical sciences.

Through teaching what they learn to one another, students discover they can become experts, speak to peers in formal settings, create resources for themselves and the school, and engage with learners of all ages. The faculty gets to discuss scientific and historical concepts and phenomena, plan activities and field trips in collaboration, and keep our teaching fresh, while tapping the materials, resources, and plans of five years before. The *Systems* DVD reproduces one of our concept planning pages: a form that helps us collect and organize ideas for teaching about each topic within a theme.

Writing plays a big role in thinking and learning across the curriculum. Students in grades K–8 write about their observations and questions in history and science notebooks. In science, they record what they learn from demonstrations, experiments, observations of, and experiences in the natural world. In history, they record, speculate about, participate in, envision, and summarize events and phenomena. "Prompts for Content-Area Writing," included on the *Systems* DVD, defines the kinds of informal writing we ask of student-researchers. In addition, children participate in dramatizations, perform role-plays, read trade books and primary sources, write songs and booklets, create art and posters, maintain timelines, take field trips, plan quests, study maps, work with experts in their fields, tour museums, summarize key ideas and information, conduct individual and small-group research projects, and make presentations to their class, other classes, the whole school, and the community beyond.

Because reading for information is a different activity than reading a story, we teach students in grades 3–8 about these two modes of reading: when the point is to disappear into a story and become lost in it, versus times when their purpose is to focus on ideas, information, and trying not to get lost. Kids need to understand that reading comprehension is different from one genre to another. "How to Read History and Science for Understanding and Retention," included on the *Systems* DVD, details the procedure our students in grades 3–8 practice when they read articles and chapters about science and history topics. Another document, "Procedures for Taking Notes on a Presentation," gives kids tips on how to attend to, record, and access the information that peers report to them about the topics they researched.

CTL teachers of 3–8 also tap research that shows that taking "tests" can actually help people recall what they've read or heard. Since learning depends on the ability to retrieve information—to organize it and create cues and connections to help access it—we give students non-stress tests that my kids named "retrieval practices." Retrieval practices consist of open-ended questions about the key facts and concepts of a reading or unit of study: no tricks, ambiguities, or picky details. They're ungraded and uncollected. Students correct their own in free-wheeling class discussions. Sometimes I'll assign a class the same retrieval practice two or three times. A sample from a history class is included on the *Systems* DVD.

Given the constructivist inclinations of the CTL faculty, we were surprised by research that showed that tests could promote learning. We were also intrigued. What we discovered is that frequent, low-key retrieval practices up the ante for students' memories, while not judging, labeling, or stressing kids, because the results are fluid and confidential. My students often create their own retrieval practices for history topics: small groups generate and submit questions, and I compile them. This process, too, is valuable. It shows me what they consider the essential data about a topic, what they've missed, and where they've gone off the rails.

Students leave CTL knowledgeable—about how past and present intersect; about the actions of individuals and groups and the influences of geography and environment in shaping the course of history and humanity; about the kept and broken promises of the United States; the biology of humans, animals, and plants; the sky above them and the waters that flow around them; and the discoveries and inventions that promote human progress and threaten it. They get to engage as researchers—read, talk, theorize, experiment, write, report, and debate. They encounter evidence-rich versions of the natural, physical, ancient, and contemporary worlds. They are curious, and they are proud of the knowledge they acquire. This seems like a lot—more than enough—to ask of a science and history curriculum.

Develop Your Own Innovations

The practices that my colleagues and I developed have been refined over years of teaching. Each began when one of us wondered, "If I tried *this*, would students get better at, understand, remember, or learn how to do *that*?"

Some Questions That Might Lead to Innovation:

- What are my students struggling with or not appreciating? Where are they growing by leaps and bounds? What accounts for the difference?
- What have I tried that seems to be working? What still doesn't work? Why not? Can I refine it? Should I abandon it? What might better engage and instruct my students?
- What are other teachers and researchers in the field suggesting to help children grow in this area? Can I read their research and adapt their methods to meet my students' needs?

Tap Resources About CTL's Innovations

The *Systems* DVD for this chapter includes guidelines for and samples of CTL innovations:

- Protocol for K–4 Reading Buddies
- What Makes a Good Discussion in a Reader's Roundtable?
- How to Write a Letter-Essay
- Sample Letter-Essay Exchange
- Sample Mathematician Biography
- Science Theme Curriculum: Woods and Wildlife
- Sample History Theme Curriculum: Immigration and the First Half of the 20th Century
- History Planning Page: The Great Depression
- Prompts for Content-Area Writing
- How to Read History and Science for Understanding and Retention
- Tips for Taking Notes on a Presentation
- Retrieval Practice on the Great Depression, Gr. 7–8

Helene Coffin's book *Every Child a Reader: Month by Month Lessons to Teach Beginning Reading* (Scholastic) provides a detailed account of how she uses poetry to teach reading. The strategies she teaches to fourth-grade reading tutors are based on Marie Clay's work, especially *The Early Detection of Reading Difficulties, Third Edition* (Heinemann).

Glenn describes his reading workshop innovations in *Reader's Roundtable: Conversations at the Core of a Reading Classroom* (forthcoming from Stenhouse). I detail the use of letter-essays in *In the Middle* (Heinemann) and *The Reading Zone* (Scholastic).

Teachers interested in writing and reading to learn history and science will be helped by *Write to Learn* by Donald Murray (Holt, Rinehart, and Winston), plus *Comprehension and Collaboration* by Stephanie Harvey and Harvey Daniels, and Thomas Newkirk's *The Art of Slow Reading*, both from Heinemann. We also love *A Place for Wonder: Reading and Writing Nonfiction in the Primary Grades* (Stenhouse) by Georgia Heard. Our favorite books for teaching American history are Joy Hakim's *A History of US*, *Volumes 1–10*, from Oxford University Press.

Protocol for K–4 Reading Buddies

(Nancie Atwell and Helene Coffin)

1. Poetry Binders
- Kindergartners read aloud to their fourth-grade buddies from their poetry binders. They start with the two new poems of the week.
- Kindergartners may then choose an old, favorite poem to read aloud. They might also talk about the illustrations they created the previous weekend.

2. Sight-Word Cards
- Fourth graders ask their buddies to read aloud to them from cards on which Helene has printed individual collections of sight words.
- If a kindergartner:
  - reads a word correctly right away, the fourth grader makes a checkmark on the card.
  - hesitates before reading a word, the fourth grader records a question mark.
  - can't read a word, the fourth grader doesn't record any symbol.
- When a sight-word card has five check marks, the fourth grader removes it from the kindergartner's collection. This word has become automatic.

3. Strategy Practice
- Kindergartners select one of the Just-Righ[t]
  gathered during reading workshop to read
  their fourth-grade buddies use the metho[d]
  wants her students to practice.

What strategies do beginning readers need
  - Where to start
  - Which way to go
  - How to return sweep back to the left
  - Word-by-word matching (each spoke[n]
  - Illustrations provide clues
  - The size and shape of a word provide[s]
  - The rest of the sentence and story pr[o]
  - The initial letters of a word provide c[lues]
  - Sometimes there are small known wo[rds]
  - Printed texts make sense

What methods can help beginning readers
  - Sit side by side or with your buddy o[n]
    the pictures. As you read, talk about t[he]
  - Touch the words as you read them, a[nd]
    them to you.

What Makes a Good Discussion in a Reader's Roundtable?

(Glenn Powers)

- **Listen**: Give your complete attention to each speaker, showing the students in your group that you value their contributions.
  - Look at each speaker.
  - Try not to fidget or doodle.
- **Respond to Group Members**: Expand on others' ideas by sharing your thoughts and feelings about what they contribute to the conversation.
  - Refer to the speaker and his or her comment.
  - Explain why you agree, and support it with evidence.
  - Explain your different opinion, and support it with evidence.
- **Ask Questions**: Inquire to better understand others' ideas:
  - Tell me more about. . . .
  - What do you mean. . . ?
  - Why do you think. . . ?
- **Share Ideas and Justify Your Opinions**: Read aloud or summarize parts of the book that demonstrate the issue you are addressing and **explain** why they are significant. Justify your opinions with evidence from the book or your own life, as appropriate. Examples:
  - I think . . . is a good example of a metaphor or symbol because. . . .
  - I wonder if the relationship between these two characters might have changed if they had. . . .
  - I was surprised that the plot changed course, because I was expecting. . .
  - This part reminds me of . . . because. . . .
  - I don't understand why the author keeps on repeating this word or phrase: . . . .
  - I like this section of writing because. . . .
  - I noticed . . . because. . . .
  - I wish . . . because. . . .
  - I think this story is really about . . . because. . . .
- **Feedback**: Consider what has been done well, by you and your classmates, as critics, and make decisions about what needs to be improved. Set goals for next time:
  - *Warm feedback* describes what the group did well in the roundtable conversation.
  - *Cool feedback* sums up what the group needs to improve on next time.

History Theme Curriculum:
Immigration and the First Half of the 20th Century

Trimester 1 Topics:

Personal History

- Family Trees and Genealogy
- Personal History Time Lines
- Cross-Generational Questionnaire
- Bio-Poems
- Grandparents' Day Activities
- Ancestor Photo Poems
- "Where I'm From" Poems à la George Ella Lyons

Immigration

- Ellis Island
- Irish
- Chinese
- Japanese
- German
- Scandinavian
- French
- Italian
- Eastern European
- Forced Emigration of Africans
- Today's "Fourth Wave"
- Contemporary Immigration an

Trimester 2 Topics:

Immigrant Roots of U.S. Holid

The Gilded Age

- Wright Brothers
- Woman Suffrage
- Panama Canal
- *Titanic*
- Child Labor
- Flu Pandemic of 1918

How to Write a Letter-Essay

(Nancie Atwell)

Dear _____ ,

Your critic's notebook is a place for you, me, and your friends to consider books, authors, and writing. You'll think about literature in informal letter-essays you write to me and to friends, and we'll write back to you about your ideas and observations. Your letter-essays and our responses will become a record of the reading, criticism, learning, and teaching we accomplished together.

Each letter-essay should be at least three pages long and written as a critical response to *one book*—in other words, not a series of paragraphs about a series of titles, but a long look at a book that intrigues you. You should write a letter-essay to me or to a friend in your critic's notebook every three weeks, due on Thursday mornings. We'll correspond in cycles: you'll write two letter-essays to me, then two to one friend of your choosing, then two to me again, and so on.

Before you write, look over your reading record. Which title would be most enjoyable to revisit as a fan? What book that you abandoned—or remained hopeful about to the bitter end—would be satisfying to revisit in a pan? Once you've decided, skim the book to refresh your memory and to find a passage you think is significant in terms of the writing—for example, the author's approach to character development, plot structure, lead or conclusion, dialogue, setting, diction, imagery, narration, reflection, and, especially, development of theme. Choose a chunk of text that you think *shows something essential* about the author's writing. Copy—or photocopy and tape in—the passage you chose, highlight its essential features, and describe what it shows about how the author wrote the book.

What else might you do in a letter-essay? Compare the author or book to another. Tell what surprised, pleased, or dissatisfied you about the writing. Pose questions. Voice your opinions about where and how the author succeeded or failed. Contemplate the genre. Rate the book (1–10), and explain your rating. Consider who else might enjoy the book. Describe what you would have done differently if you were the author. And always, always, describe the themes that emerge, through the characters and their story.

Once you've written your letter-essay, hand-deliver your critic's notebook to your correspondent. If that's me, put it in my rocking chair on Thursday morning. When a friend gives you his or her notebook, you must answer in at least paragraph length by Monday morning. After you've written back, hand-deliver your friend's notebook—don't put it in his or her locker or backpack. You may not lose or damage someone's critic's notebook.

Date your letter-essays in the upper-right-hand corner, and use a conventional greeting (*Dear* _____ ,) and closing (*Love, Your friend, Sincerely,* etc.). Cite the author's full name and the book title in the first paragraph; after that, use the author's last name only. Indicate the title by capitalizing and underlining it—for example, *The Outsiders* by S. E. Hinton.

I look forward to thinking about literature with you in this serious-but-friendly way. I can't wait for your first letter-essay and a year of opportunities to learn from you, learn with you, and help you learn more about the power and pleasures of good writing.

Love,
Nancie

Science Theme Curriculum: Woods and Wildlife

Trimester 1 Topics:

Trees

- parts of a tree
- types of trees
- types of leaves
- tree and leaf identification
- how to measure trees
- life cycle of trees
- forest succession
- tree zones and habitats
- tree products

Field Trips and Presentations:

- Biscay Orchard
- Viles Arboretum, Augusta
- Damariscotta River Association
- Oven's Mouth
- Dodge Point
- Hidden Valley Nature Center
- Singing Meadows
- CTL Woods

Trimester 2 Topics:

Mammals of Maine

- characteristics
- food, habitat, and adaptions
- animal track and scat identification
- mammals in winter: hibernate, do
  or active
- balance of nature: predators, prey,
  and food chain
- tooth dentition and types
- types of adaptations: physical, beh
  and reproductive

Trees in Winter

- identification in winter: bark,
  buds (terminal and lateral), odor,

Sample History Planning Page: The Great Depression

"STUDENTS ARE IN A CONSTANT STATE OF SELF-ASSESSMENT AS THEY CONSIDER WHERE THEY'VE BEEN, WHO THEY ARE, WHERE THEY MIGHT GO NEXT, WHAT THEY DON'T UNDERSTAND YET, AND WHAT THEY NEED TO KNOW."

8

Student Self-Assessment

Talk About It and Reflect

- What are all the different kinds of assessment you use? How effective would you say each one is in promoting the goal of individual growth?

- Describe any ways that your students evaluate their own work, progress, and goals. How do you think their insights might inform your assessments and their intentions?

- Have you ever considered partnering with your students to communicate their progress to parents? What advantages might there be in adding a child's voice to the reporting process?

- How familiar are you with portfolios—representative collections of student work—as a basis for evaluating and communicating a child's progress?

Read About Portfolios and Student-Led Evaluation Conferences

CTL provides a potent combination of rich instruction, opportunities for kids to take initiative as they put what they learn into practice, and occasions for them to talk and write about their academic experiences, including what they might do differently the next time. Students develop skills and habits of mind that allow them to be productive, learn from their successes, and, when something doesn't go well, learn from their mistakes. Reflection, self-evaluation, and goal-setting ensure growth.

Our students evaluate their work and progress in a formal way in every subject area at the end of each trimester. But informal self-assessment is a continuous process, as we ask children, across the disciplines and all day long, "What are you working on? How's it going? What have you learned so far? What stumbling blocks did you encounter? What did you try? How did that work? How can I help you?" Students are in a constant state of self-assessment as they consider where they've been, where they are, where they might go next, what they don't understand yet, and what they need to know.

At the end of each trimester, my colleagues and I stop teaching for a week. We invite students to pause, reflect, write and talk about their work of the previous twelve weeks, and make plans for the trimester to come. Every class in every subject area becomes an evaluation workshop, as children examine collections of their work, make or request photocopies of selected examples, complete self-assessment questionnaires, and assemble the contents of their portfolios.

Portfolios are three-ring binders with plastic sleeves inside that display students' self-evaluation questionnaires, captioned photocopies of their record-keeping forms, and samples of their writing, responses to books and poems, spelling, and work as mathematicians, historians, scientists, and

Portfolio Preparation in Glenn's Group

artists. Children also mount and sleeve photographs that the teachers have taken of their learning in action. We give our students lists of what their portfolios should include, trimester to trimester.

One objective in using portfolios is for kids to create a body of evidence—a basis for analyzing their processes, products, challenges, growth, and goals. The self-assessment questionnaires we design each trimester give them a prism for examining their evidence, reflecting on it, and establishing goals for their work. We've found that when students don't write about their learning, they lose the thread. The best way to formalize knowledge and make it long-lasting is for kids to write. Self-evaluation questionnaires and the captions students compose about the contents of their portfolios give them the opportunity to describe and consolidate their learning.

Only after students have evaluated themselves do teachers step in as evaluators. Self-assessment is that important. When a child's portfolio is complete, the teacher uses it as one basis for writing a progress report that details the student's accomplishments, challenges, and goals. The goals we list on the progress report are coauthored: a combination of the objectives the student named in his or her self-assessment and other goals the teacher has observed the child needs to tackle, subject area by subject area.

The teacher also creates a summary of the whole-class activities of the trimester—the mini-lessons, discussions, projects, field trips, readings, and so forth. My students each highlight a copy of the trimester summary, indicating what was most useful to them, so parents can enjoy the benefit of their child's governing gaze when they review the list. Both documents, the progress report and the summary of activities, become part of a student's permanent records.

When CTL teachers began to experiment with portfolios, we presented them to our students' parents during evaluation conferences, sans our students, and it felt beyond inauthentic. Here was a body of work an author had created, but we teachers were sitting in the author's chair. So we shifted course and invited the children to lead their evaluation conferences. We never looked back.

Our students present their best versions of themselves when they sit down with us and their parents. We ask them to go deep and be deep as researchers of their learning. Our highest praise for a portfolio is that it is interesting. Of course, we also nudge students to write a lot, demonstrate the range of what they've learned, and use the vocabulary of the disciplines to name their understandings and insights.

Teachers open a student-teacher-parent conference by telling parents, "Your child is excited to tell you the story of this trimester." Then the student turns the pages and presents the material in the portfolio—reads it, describes it, lays claim to his or her growth, and assesses it using the lexicon of each subject. Afterward, the teacher reads or summarizes the progress report and the child's goals for the subsequent trimester. The conference closes with the teacher asking, "Do you have any questions or observations, for me or your child?" Parents take the portfolios home to peruse and show grandparents. We ask that they be returned to school within two weeks.

Because the end of the school year is such a frantic time, CTL teachers don't schedule evaluation conferences in June. Rather, students compile their portfolios, and then they and their teachers coauthor an extensive report that provides a portrait of the child as a learner at the completion of the school year. It consists of a student's summative self-assessment in writing, reading, and mathematics, accompanied by the teacher's observations of the child's strengths, along with a final list of goals he or she needs to work toward the following September.

CTL teachers assess and report the progress children achieve toward their goals, but we do not assign grades. In my previous teaching situation, where I also taught writing and reading in a workshop setting, I was required to assign letter grades. I based them on the degree to which a student had achieved his or her goals. This meant that a student who had met all of his or her objectives for writing received an A. Solid progress earned a B. I assigned a C for fair or adequate progress, a D for little progress, and, although it never happened, an F for zero progress. Parents and students perceived this as a fair, objective evaluation system. It reflected what students were being asked to do every day in my classroom, and the evidence for a grade was apparent in the contents of a student's writing folder, reading records, and literary letters.

The assessment scheme we've implemented at CTL provides a detailed picture of a student's abilities, activities, growth, and challenges. It reflects what happens day-to-day in our classes. It involves parents in a meaningful—often delightful—way. The information it conveys to mothers, fathers, and the next year's teacher is specific and *useful*. It's individualized and goal oriented, and the goals are based on the observations of a professional teacher, in collaboration with the learner. It holds students accountable. And it begins with their judgments about what they know, can do, have done, and need to do next. I can't imagine a more worthwhile use of our time as teachers, or our students' as learners, when it comes to evaluating progress and nurturing growth.

When we transform our classes into workshops, we send kids unmistakable signals about the importance of initiative, commitment, and reflection. Making assessment an occasion for students to analyze their work, set goals, and describe progress extends and enriches their growth. It affords a crucial perspective for teachers to learn about our students' learning. And it strengthens what happens in the workshop across all the days and weeks of a school year.

Watch Portfolio Preparation and Student-Led Evaluation Conferences

Although we pause in our teaching of new content at the end of a trimester and focus class time on student self-assessment and portfolio preparation, teachers don't sit back and observe. Our role is to provide guidelines and guidance. Notice how teachers conduct evaluation minilessons and meet with individuals as other members of the group research their learning and consult their records, files, binders, and class notes.

We filmed two student-parent-teacher evaluation conferences. Nicco, a third grader, is an old hand at this, while Avery, a seventh grader, is new to CTL. This is his

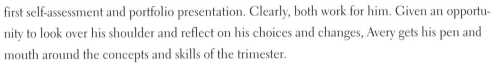

first self-assessment and portfolio presentation. Clearly, both work for him. Given an opportunity to look over his shoulder and reflect on his choices and changes, Avery gets his pen and mouth around the concepts and skills of the trimester.

Note how the format is the same: each student reads, explains, and describes. He doesn't read the answers to all the self-assessment questions—there's too much data for a 45-minute meeting. At the completion of portfolio preparation, each class determines which questions and answers they'll share at the conference, and which parents can read when the portfolios go home. Also notice that conferences begin with students' voices and goals. Teachers follow up with our observations and objectives. The final goals are specific, pertinent, and achievable.

At the middle-school level, students and their parents move among Sally Macleod (science), Katie Rittershaus (math), and me (writing, reading, and history). Normally we're stationed in three different rooms. For the purposes of filming a 7–8 evaluation conference, we moved to Avery and his parents.

Develop Your Own Student Self-Assessments

- At the end of the grading period, review your lesson plans. Take notes on subject area emphases and key ideas. Use these as the basis for open-ended questions that ask students to show what they know, remember, think, value, and can do.

- Except for math—where students will need sufficient space to demonstrate computational strategies—and the final, coauthored report in June, keep the self-assessment questionnaire to a manageable length of one to three pages. Don't require complete sentences. We push our kids hard for data and specifics, so we favor lists. Students can hide a lack of knowledge amidst paragraphs of long sentences, but bulleted lists cut to the chase.

- In writing and reading, begin with questions that ask students to survey their work—range and productivity—and articulate their literary criteria. Ask writers about number of pieces completed, genres represented, which piece is best, and why: what did the child do in crafting it that makes it a success? In reading, ask about the number of books read, genres represented, best book and poems, and what the authors and poets did in crafting them. Answers to these questions are useful to kids and teachers in prompting observations about changes in productivity, pace, preferences, versatility, stamina, habits, and standards for effective writing in many genres.

- In the questions that follow, address the focuses of the marking period, the ones you noted in your plan book. In the fall, I tend to ask overarching questions about all the ways a student has changed so far, as a writer and reader. I want kids to learn how to step back and reflect on the big picture of themselves. Plus, beginning-of-the-year changes are *noticeable*: it's encouraging to students to name them and see how much they've already grown.

- End the self-assessment with questions about students' plans for the next grading period. Ask them to set goals as writers in such areas as productivity, spelling, mastery of conventions, elements of process and craft, and work in genres. In reading, target pace, book selections, experiments with authors and genres, written responses to books, and participation in discussions and as booktalkers. In history and science, request their goals as a reader of information, researcher, and participant in discussions and activities.

- If you use portfolios, create a checklist for each subject area, to ensure that it's a representative collection. Assign students to caption each inclusion with an explanation of how it reflects their knowledge, opinions, criteria, or growth.

- If you don't use portfolios, still consider a self-assessment questionnaire—the process is that informative and worthwhile. Attach to it copies of key samples of a student's work so that parents can glean a basis for their child's reflections and goals.

- With younger children—kindergarten and grade one—take dictation if their invented spelling isn't decipherable. CTL teachers send out requests for parent volunteers to help us interview young children and record their responses on the self-assessment questionnaires.

Tap Resources About Student Self-Assessment at CTL

The *Systems* DVD is packed with samples of portfolio checklists, self-assessment questionnaires, and student responses. I've included a range of grade levels and subject areas. Notice the similarities, K–8. CTL teachers value evidence, analysis, reflection, and goal-setting.

- Portfolio Checklist, Kindergarten
- Portfolio Checklist, Grades 3–4
- Portfolio Checklist, Grades 7–8 Mathematics
- Portfolio Checklist, Grades 7–8 Writing, Reading, and History
- Writing Self-Evaluation, Kindergarten
- Math Self-Evaluation, Kindergarten
- Reading Self-Evaluation, Kindergarten
- Writing Self-Evaluation, Grades 3–4
- Math Self-Evaluation, Grades 3–4
- Reading Self-Evaluation, Grades 3–4
- History Self-Evaluation, Grades 3–4
- Science Self-Evaluation, Grades 3–4
- Writing Self-Evaluation, Grades 7–8
- Reading Self-Evaluation, Grades 7–8
- History Self-Evaluation, Grades 7–8
- Math Self-Evaluation, Grades 7–8
- Science Self-Evaluation, Grades 7–8
- Final Self-Evaluation in Writing, Kindergarten
- Final Self-Evaluation in Math, Kindergarten
- Final Self-Evaluation in Writing and Reading, Grades 7–8
- Nicco's Writing Self-Evaluation
- Jill's Report on Third Grader Nicco

- Avery's Self-Evaluation in Writing

- Nancie's Report on Seventh-Grader Avery in Writing, Reading, and History

- Nancie's Summary of First-Trimester Minilessons, Activities, and Discussions

- Katie's Report on Avery in Math

- Sally's Report on Avery in Science

Portfolio Checklist, Kindergarten

(Helene Coffin)

Reading Section

Student Photos:

___ Reading a poetry chart

___ Reading a poem from the anthology

___ Engaged in a word study

___ Reading the class message

___ Independently reading a just-right book

___ Reading a book with reading buddy

___ Practicing sight words with reading buddy

___ Reviewing poetry anthology with reading buddy

Student Work:

___ Reading record

___ Favorite poem

___ High-frequency word list

___ Self-evaluation

Writing Section

Student Photos:

___ Sharing from the class mascot journal

___ Telling a story during storytelling

___ Writing text in a story booklet

___ Illustrating text in a story booklet

___ Working with an ABC chart or words from our word wall

___ Practicing letter formation

Student Work:

___ Writing record

___ Published story or poem

___ Draft of a story or poem

___ Letter formation page

___ Best sketchbook page

___ Self-evaluation

Math Section

Student Photos:

___ Working in a large group on math concepts

___ Working in a small group on math concepts

___ Working independently on math concepts

___ Working in math journal

___ Using cooking tools
 (grater, sifter, measuring devices, etc.)

Student Work:

___ Samples of student work representing covered math concepts

___ Calendar page

___ Math self-evaluation

Science and History Section

Student Photos:

___ Working in large groups (field trips, collaborations, etc.)

___ Working with partners and class (projects and other hands-on activities, plus read-alouds)

___ Working independently

Student Work:

___ Independent work

___ Self-evaluation
 (Trimester 1 and Trimester 2 only)

Other Section:

___ Photos of special events and highlights (Pumpkin Planting, Field Day, Holiday Program, Spring Program, special cultural events, kindergarten celebrations, recess activities, phys. ed., music, art, birthdays, first lost teeth, etc.)

Reading Self-Evaluation, Kindergarten

(Helene Coffin)

Name: _____

1. What do good readers do when they come to words they don't

 * _____

 * _____

 * _____

2. How do you figure out words you don't know?

 _____

 _____

3. Which two reading activities did you *enjoy* the most?

 Reading Poems on Charts ___ Sight-Word Practice

 Reading Just-Right Books ___ Reading with Helene

 Building Words ___ Recording Predictions

 Reading Aloud a Favorite Picture Book to the Class

4. Which two reading activities *helped* you most, to become a be

 Reading Poems on Charts ___ Sight-Word Practice

 Reading Just-Right Books ___ Reading with Helene

 Building Words ___ Recording Predictions

5. How have these activities helped to improve your reading?

 _____

6. Name a Just-Right book you read that you enjoyed. What was the best part of the story? Why?

 _____

 _____

 _____

Katie's Report on Avery in Math

Avery
Grade 7 Progress Report
November

Katherine A. Rittershaus
Teacher, 7th/8th Grade Mathematics
Center for Teaching and Learning

Accomplishments

- Solid understanding of the coordinate grid: can accurately locate points, and calculate distances
- Strong understanding of how to find the area and perimeters of plane figures drawn on dot grids with whole-number vertices
- Understands square roots as the lengths of the sides of squares
- Mastered the Pythagorean theorem and how it relates the areas of the squares on the sides of a right triangle; can use it to solve all related problems
- Explored and has a strong understanding of the special properties of 30°- 60°- 90° and 45°- 45°- 90° right triangles
- Investigated and understands rational numbers written as decimals and irrational numbers as non-terminating, non-repeating decimals
- Explored and understands the particular relationships of the slopes of perpendicular and parallel lines
- Explored and can find irrational slopes and knows how to represent them on a coordinate grid
- Covered language of comparison statements and formed common types of comparison statements about data: fractions, percents, ratios, and differences
- Understands scaling problems and has developed strategies for scaling ratios to make comparisons or find missing parts of equivalent ratios
- Can write and solve proportions
- Strong understanding of how to write and find two types of unit rates
- Through *Data Around Us* has developed a broader understanding of numbers, can use benchmarks, and express numbers, large and small, in scientific notation and vice versa
- Introduced to the different units of measure, customary and metric
- To date has compiled a neat and complete 50-word vocabulary resource. Avery always completes this assignment on time with sh[...] clear definitions and accompanying detailed examples
- Kept an excellent record of his class work in the journal section of [...] math binder. His work is neat and easy to follow. He answers que[...] fully and completely
- Completed over 30 daily brush-ups, averaging a 3.7 out of 5 [...]

Goals

- Should review previously defined words in word wall and add any additional information that you've learned since first defining the term
- For definitions in word wall write more expansively about what you understand so that they truly reflect what you know
- Keep all homework logs until the trimester ends so they can serve as a writing resource for self-evaluations
- Write more daily reflections and have them follow the class work each day
- Take time to check over work
- Continue to practice problems involving order of operations and scientific notation
- Review how to tell the difference between two types of rational numbers: terminating and repeating

---

Writing Self-Evaluation, Kindergarten

(Helene Coffin)

Name: _____

1. List the things that good writers do when they write.

  • _____

  • _____

  • _____

2. How have you improved as a writer since the first day of kindergarten?

  • _____

  • _____

  • _____

3. List what you need to work on to make your writing easier to read and underst[...]

  • _____

  • _____

  • _____

4. List what you have learned to do as an illustrator.

  • _____

  • _____

  • _____

5. List how you could improve your illustrations.

  • _____

  • _____

  • _____

Nicco's Writing Self-Evaluation

Jill Cotta
Center for Teaching and Learning

Writing Self-Evaluation
Trimester 1

Name Nicco   Grade 3 Date 11-16

1. How many pieces of writing did you finish this trimester? 6

2. What is your best piece of writing? *Explain why.*
Pumpkin
• I used descriptive words.
• I used strong verbs.
• I used words that made my readers feel like they're with me carving the pumpkin.

3. What is your favorite poem we discussed from our poetry anthologies? *Why? What did the poet do?*
The pond by Charlotte Zolotow
• The poet compared ripples in the water to blue ribbons. • She compares the lake at night to a bowl of black ink.

4. What do you do to write good free-verse poetry? *Please list.*
• I use strong words.
• I use descriptive verbs.
• I use words that make movies in my audience's mind.

5. What do you do well as a writer? *List your strengths.*
• I use strong descriptive words.
• I use words that make my readers feel they're there with me.
• I use verbs so that I describe what I'm trying to say.

6. What would you like to do better as a writer? *List your goals.*
• I would like to be able to write poems with comparisons.
• I would like to write poems that make my readers feel/sad
• I would like to write poems with feeling.

7. What do you look for when you proofread your writing for conventions? *Please list.*
• I look for words that I don't think I have spelled correctly.
• I look for punctuation marks.
• I look for capital letters.

Nancie's Report on Seventh Grader Avery in Writing, Reading, and History

1st Trimester Progress Report

Student: _Avery_   Grade: _7_   Teacher: _Nancie Atwell_

ACCOMPLISHMENTS, STRENGTHS, and CHALLENGES   **GOALS**

Writing and Spelling / Emphases: *Writing Territories, Techniques of Free-Verse Poetry, the Rule of "So What?" or Theme, the Two-Day Walk-Away, How and Why to Edit, CTL's Spelling Study Process, The Rule of Thoughts and Feelings, Writing off the Page, Monthly Spelling Reviews, The Rule of Write about a Pebble, Where Poems Hide in Everyday Life, Parody, and Techniques of Effective Memoirs*

- A productive trimester, in terms of growth and quantity: six poems in his own, a collaborative parody w classmates, and substantial progress on a memoir
- Began to use + view writing as self-expression, vs. performance, i.e., focused on his life + experiences, crafted them, and developed themes: this is just right.
- Experimented richly with writing off-the-page and is developing a full, mature writing process.
- Takes every lesson and conference and runs with it, plus has started to glean from the lit he reads, esp. poetry. Sets high standards for himself and is collecting a repertoire of techniques to help him achieve them: per small reflections, cadence, sensory verbs + adjectives, line + stanza breaks, + concrete specifics, but esp. theme.
- Spelling is solid – probably 98% correct on drafts – as are conventions of usage, apart from comma glitches.
- An impelled writer; always on task; his confidence grows in knowledge + experience.

Goals:
- Draft more on weekends – at least two pages?
- Beware of unnecessary punctuation at ends of lines of poems
- Keep an I presence in poems, and revise for sensory imagery and concrete specifics.
- Brainstorm titles at the end of the process.
- Experiment off-the-page with alternative conclusions.
- Be on the lookout for clichés + ineffective repetition.
- In narratives, shoot for a balance of dialogue, action, reflection, + description.

Reading / Emphases: *Poems That Demonstrate the Versatility of the Free-Verse Genre, Someday Books, Booktalks, Glossary of Poetic Terms, Literary Vocabulary, National Banned Books Week, Letter-Essays about Literature, Poems about Growing Up, Reading of Students' First Poems of 2010-11, the Popularity of Young Adult Novels among Literary Adults, Psycholinguistic Reading Theory, William Carlos Williams' Poetry and Influence, Memoir as a Genre, and Memorable Children's Picture Books*

- Finished thirteen books representing five genres: a great start. Favorite was the adult memoir *Rocket Boys* by Homer Hickam Jr.; also found much y.a. fiction he loved by such fine writers as Patrick Ness, Suzanne Collins, + Ned Vizzini.
- Became obsessed w a new genre, dystopian scifi: a smart, appropriate choice. Rejected thrillers and is in the process of leaving most fantasy behind. Is starting to perceive the differences between popular and literary fiction.
- Comprehension, vocabulary, and pace are all solid.
- Is learning vocab. of criticism; contributions to class discussions of lit are less personal ("I like this poem b/c it's funny") and more analytical: comments about sensory im him, concrete specifics, cadence, compression, figurative language, persona, theme, caesuras, + other experiments w for
- His letter-essays have moved from enthusiastic plot synopses to considerations of "the basics": theme and the author's style. Again, this is just right.

History / Emphases: *the War in Iraq, the Mid-Term Elections, Review of the B Pemaquid, George Waymouth's 1605 Expedition to Maine, the Pilgrims' 1620 Tra Colony of 1607-8, Jamestown, Plymouth, Techniques for Notetaking, Techniques Reading to Learn and Remember*

- Avery demonstrates some good understandings of early Eng. colonies in his self-eval., along with a few confusions and areas where he missed his big ideas + focused on side issues. In general he reads and retains history well. His history notes are excellent – he aced the open-notebook test – and formatted so they're useful to him. He's an enthusiastic participant in every kind of activity and discussion and is fascinated by current po events and more recent American history.

© 2014 by Nancie Atwell from *Systems to Transform Your Classroom and S*

Sally's Report on Avery in Science

Sally Macleod   Center for Teaching and Learning
FIRST TRIMESTER SCIENCE PROGRESS REPORT
Student: _Avery_   Grade: _7_   Date: _11-26_

ACCOMPLISHMENTS, STRENGTHS, and CHALLENGES   **GOALS**

HISTORY OF THE GEOLOGICAL EARTH

Avery focused on the movement and creation of land masses for our class timeline project. He has a good understanding of the basic patterns of change through the residual evidence that helps distinguish eons, eras, and periods. He worked through challenges calculating a reasonable scale and estimating vast amounts of time.

EARTH'S COMPOSITION

Avery can identify similarities and differences among earth's layers.
He has recorded information about earth's composition, based on temperature, pressure, state, and distance from the surface.

PLATE TECTONICS AND CONTINENTAL DRIFT

Avery has participated in activities that represented small-scale plate movement and related the outcomes to a global scale and continental drift.

PHYSICAL PROPERTIES OF ROCKS AND MINERALS

Avery earnestly worked through rock and mineral observation, experimentation, and calculations to identify some of the unknown samples presented to him.
He relies on adult verification before accepting his own work.

LABORATORY

Avery is a persistent scientist, always working toward an end.
He participates in all lab activities and writes thorough lab reports on time.
Remember that write ups can be excellent, even with unexpected or poor/inconclusive results.

Goals:
- Be aware of the processes involved in teamwork.
- check details in your notes and readings for accuracy.
- start to relate earth's history to its layers and chemical composition.
- Details will fit into a big picture or a theory if you delve.
- start to look for evidence of change.
- Use details as support for theory, instead of stating details for their own sake.
- Relate details such as density or hardness to overall attributes of rocks.
- Trust your work.
- Spend more time on the process
- work on the individual components of a lab report. Be sure the procedure is repeatable but not tedious!

© 2014 by Nancie Atwell from *Systems to Transform Your Classroom and School*. Portsmouth, NH: Heinemann.

First Trimester Conference Notes

Jill Cotta
Center for Teaching and Learning

Student: Nicco   **Grade:** 3   **Date:** November

ACCOMPLISHMENTS, STRENGTHS, AND CHALLENGES	GOALS
• Counts money and records amounts using a dollar sign and decimal point; sometimes places the dollar sign to the right by the cents instead of to the left by the dollar amount.	
History and Science	
• Charts, maps, and graphs are neat and detailed. • Understands the key concepts of this trimester's science topics. • Understands the key concepts of the founding of Jamestown, Popham, and Plymouth. • Uses notes and other printed material to add detail when explaining key concepts.	• Take on an individual project when he finishes an assignment early.

Jill's Report on Third Grader Nicco

First Trimester Conference Notes

Jill Cotta
Center for Teaching and Learning

Student: Nicco   **Grade:** 3   **Date:** November

ACCOMPLISHMENTS, STRENGTHS, AND CHALLENGES	GOALS
Personal and Social Development	
• Has a great sense of humor; dry. • Takes his work seriously; wants to do his best job. • Works well independently and with partners. • Usually volunteers ideas in group discussions; needs to contribute more frequently. • Chooses good seats in the meeting area when reminded. • Often sits outside the circle in the meeting area and is not facing the chart.	• Volunteer ideas to discussions more frequently. • Independently choose good seats in the meeting area to limit distractions. • Be part of the circle and face the chart in the meeting area.
Reading	
• Finished sixteen books this trimester. • Chose *The Gravity Keeper* as his favorite book; liked the way the author introduced the characters. • Chooses Just Right books independently; keeps his reading record up to date. • Very focused during independent reading time especially when he chooses a good seat. • Booktalked the *Yggyssey*; summary was a bit brief; needed more detail.	• Add more detail to booktalks to interest others in the book. • Always choose a place free of distractions to sit during independent reading time.
Writing	
• Finished four pieces of writing this trimester. • Named "Pumpkin" as his best piece; used descriptive words; included a simile. • Uses his heart map and writing territories list to choose topics. • Needs help to focus topics. • Revises to add strong verbs and descriptive words with help. • Worked on placing line breaks after little phrases and punctuation.	• Continue work on focusing pieces. • Continue working on placement of line breaks.
Math	
• Completes up to 28 addition facts with sums over ten in one minute; records scores on a bar graph. • Understands place value to the hundred thousands place; knows the value of the digit in each place. • Reads and writes numbers to the hundred thousands; needs help writing those with zero as a placeholder. • Adds and subtracts larger numbers with regrouping. • Recognizes acute, obtuse, and right angles and can measure them with a simple protractor; can name many kinds of polygons.	• Practice addition and subtraction facts to increase speed. • Practice writing numbers to the hundred thousands—particularly those with zero as a placeholder. • Practice writing money amounts with a dollar sign and decimal point.

"ALTHOUGH ASSESSING WHAT'S GOING ON WITH OUR KIDS AND METHODS IS A FREQUENT FOCUS OF THE LUNCHTIME MEETINGS, WE ASSESS OURSELVES, INFORMALLY AND FORMALLY, THROUGHOUT THE DAY AND YEAR."

9

Teacher Talk and Self-Assessment

Talk About It and Reflect

- How much time do you have at school to talk with colleagues about teaching? Is it regular time or more likely a conversation in the hallway before or after school?

- When teachers at your school do gather, how would you characterize the content of the conversation? How would you change it if you could?

- What opportunities do teachers at your school have to evaluate themselves, to set professional goals or discuss them with colleagues? What might be gained, by you and your students, if specific goals that you set for yourself were an integral part of your annual evaluation?

Read About Teacher Talk and Self-Assessment

CTL teachers meet every day at 12:30. We supervise our students' lunches at noon and then send them outdoors for recess, where they're watched over by helping teachers. Our professional conversations take place in one of the classrooms, all of us squeezed around a table as we unwrap our sandwiches and talk, listen, and move ourselves and our school forward.

It's only a half an hour, but meeting every day means we accomplish most of the business of running the school in a timely, responsive fashion. We plan collaborative activities, talk about the children who concern and delight us, raise and ponder questions about methods, consider resources and field trips, adjust the schedule, set the calendar, despair over the budget, discuss professional readings, and establish and revise school policies.

When Donald Graves first visited CTL, years ago, he said, "I've never been in a school where teachers have so much time to talk to one another." And it was *half an hour*. But that half an hour makes all the difference in terms of collegiality and professional growth. A teacher isn't thinking, "Gosh, maybe I'll bring this up at next week's meeting." Instead, when something has happened and there's a sense of urgency, we know we can discuss it at lunch and, often, generate a solution. I can't stress enough how important it is for teachers to have freed-up time to talk. We keep our momentum as a school because issues don't get put on hold. Problems get noticed, talked about, and solved.

The lunch meetings don't have a set format. When I have an administrative issue, I start the discussion. Often Jill, who is CTL's head teacher for history and science, takes the lead. When one of us is concerned about a student's behavior, we talk about our observations, and the others offer their ideas. When we self-evaluated as a school in order to renew our certification, we talked off and on all that year about the curriculum and management of the school. We've engaged in heady conversations around that small round table about portfolios, mathematics instruction, multiculturalism, the Common Core Standards, the future of the school, and our particular interests as teacher-researchers—professional conversations that would not happen without our half an hour.

Teaching can be lonely—to be the adult in a room full of children all day long, with few opportunities to put your head together with those of other adults and achieve some perspective. Because of our common vision, posture as teacher-researchers, and lunchtime meetings, teaching at CTL isn't lonely. If teachers want students to have a sense of belonging to something that's bigger than they are, it's essential that we feel that way, too. At CTL, we are way too many bodies squeezed around one table every noontime because it *matters*.

Although assessing what's going on with our kids and methods is a frequent focus of the lunchtime meetings, we assess ourselves, informally and formally, throughout the day and year.

Students Loaded Up with Books Borrowed for Summer Reading

Every afternoon before she heads home, Helene looks back at her day with the kindergartners and writes about it. Jill keeps teaching notebooks, Glenn is always writing to himself on his laptop, and I cover my planbook every night with notes about what worked, what didn't, and what I need to do tomorrow.

In terms of developing a formal system of teacher assessment, it took me a while to understand that instead of me observing a class and writing a report, the same model that proved so productive for kids could be productive for their teachers, too. Given opportunities to reflect on our teaching, set goals, and discuss them, members of the CTL faculty have come up with professional objectives more specific, pertinent, and significant than I could have created in a hundred days of observations.

Every September we schedule a Monday in-service day. An hour or so is devoted to collaborative planning around the new history and science themes for the year, and the rest to teacher self-assessment. Our self-assessment questionnaire calls on us to generate goals and to evaluate the progress we made toward the goals of the previous year.

We bring completed drafts of the questionnaires to the meeting, where each teacher meets with a support team comprised of two colleagues. Category by category, we describe our challenges and intentions, field questions, and make observations and suggestions. We make ourselves vulnerable, learn from one another, hold ourselves responsible, and, goal by goal, improve our teaching.

Then, in January and again in April, we spend two or three luncheon meetings reviewing our goals—talking about how we're doing, what's working, what isn't, whether we've changed course, and why. I've been teaching for forty years, and every fall I set new goals for myself or refine old ones. I love self-assessment. It keeps my teaching fresh and nudges me to reflect on my kids, analyze my methods, conserve and refine old ones, author new ones, and take responsibility for my teaching at ever-higher levels.

I don't know of another school where professional evaluation begins with the professionals. In the case of a new CTL teacher, I do observe his or her instruction on multiple occasions in early fall and spring. I precede each visit with a conversation about the teacher's plans and goals for the lesson. Then I record my observations, impressions, and any suggestions for improvement, and the new teacher and I meet and talk. The notes of my observation go into the new hire's personnel file, along with his or her self-evaluation questionnaire and support-team comments. First-year teachers are expected to take advantage of their own goals, colleagues' comments, and my observations to improve their instruction. Their teaching always improves, because mentoring and intentionality are built into the process.

Watch Teacher Talk

The clip shows an abridged version of our lunchtime gathering on the day we began the bill of rights discussion at morning meeting. Notice the tone. It's light and collegial—we're all on the same team. And notice the diversity of topics. The faculty considers and accomplishes a lot before it's time to ring the bell that ends recess. We:

- debrief about the bill of rights debate,
- make a plan for the next constitutional convention, five years hence,
- review a second draft of a proposed school calendar,
- vote on the cover designs that students submitted to adorn the next *Acorns*, our school literary magazine,
- plant a seed, via Glenn, for a collaboration between CTL and a local nature conservancy, which led to his fifth and sixth graders spending forty school days in the woods during the "woods and wildlife" science theme year, and
- launch a new initiative to address the problem of students who don't read in the summer and lose months of measured ability because they lack access to books.

Develop Your Own Teacher Self-Assessment

- Estimate how much time you spend each week, month, and year at faculty meetings. What gets accomplished? Could some information be communicated via e-mail rather than in person?

- Could a portion of faculty meeting time be dedicated to focused teacher talk? What would happen if school leaders asked teachers to inform the agenda?

- There's immeasurable value in collaborative reflection. How might you carve out regular time to meet and talk with a colleague or a group of like-minded teachers?

- If you were to assess yourself, what goals would you set toward improving your methods for teaching, professionalism, and relationships with students, parents, and colleagues? Could teacher self-assessment become a part of the evaluation scheme at your school?

Tap Resources About Teacher Assessment

The *Systems* DVD features two versions of teacher self-assessment. The first is our original questionnaire, as completed by Helene Coffin at the start of her twenty-eighth year in the classroom. It is thoughtful, thorough, useful to her as a teacher, and beneficial to the children entrusted to her care. Although the questions are somewhat general, her answers aren't. They represent the specific plans and reflections of a long-experienced professional, one with developed intentions and deep knowledge of how to teach reading, writing, and math to kindergartners.

The second self-assessment, a recent revision, looks to the future, as the old guard begins to retire and we seek to preserve the essence of CTL. Rather than assuming that newbies have internalized a thoroughgoing understanding of the tenets of the school, the revised questionnaire asks teachers how they'll interpret and perpetuate its principles, procedures, and workshop methods. At the same time, the new self-assessment encourages the innovations that make teaching at CTL a creative, responsive process.

Conclusion

One June, three pieces of writing crossed my desk at school. The first was a note from Alison, a CTL alum who had just graduated from Harvard. She relayed a conversation with a boy who was in her class at both schools. "Niall and I were discussing just the other day how CTL, its philosophy, and the way that it taught us independence, fearlessness, and joy in learning have shaped our academic careers. I doubt that many students can so easily or directly trace their successes in college back to experiences in elementary school, but CTL kids can."

Next was a note from Denise, a parent. She thanked CTL for "the mutuality of respect, dedication, work, and support that makes this school the place that allows [students] to grow into such interesting, brave, and confident people."

Finally, there was a draft of an eighth-grade graduation speech written by Abe, Denise's son. He observed, "I don't know if a school could have given me a greater gift than decision-making skills. Everything about CTL just spoke of academic, and, therefore, future choices that will be mine to make. Every time Ted, Jill, Glenn, or Nancie said "Choose a book" or "What do you want to write about?" was a moment when I made a decision, guided by a knowledge-able person who showed me how to do so. Every time Katie or Sally said, in math or science, "Write down what you think," they were *letting me think*, preparing me for when what I write down will *really* matter…. I can tell you now, with confidence, that I can do whatever I want when I grow up."

Alison, Niall, Denise, and Abe identified and celebrated habits of mind, work, and character that are founded on engagement and experience. Such traits as independence, courage, self-confidence, and the ability to make and learn from decisions are the underground curriculum at CTL.

Our kids understand that intellectual growth involves trial and success *and* trial and error. When a decision doesn't pan out or an answer is wrong—when a self-selected book turns out to be poorly written, when they miss a key image in the poem they're trying to unpack, when they reverse steps while trying to solve an equation—they learn how to reflect on the experience and how to bounce back. Perseverance and resilience are essential components of growth, for kids *and* for their teachers.

We need to be brave—to forge ahead with the kinds of changes that can make big differences for our students. Invite children to choose, read, and talk about books, lots of them, without a quiz or book report in sight. Show them what you do when you draft a letter or poem, solve an equation, or read about history. Endeavor to make conversation and writing your primary modes of instruction, because students who make choices need opportunities to talk and write about how they turn out. Create and nurture a deliberate culture, one with traditions, rituals, in-jokes, and a bill of rights. Most important of all, take a page from Vivian Paley and tell kids, "You can't say you can't play." Walk that talk with students all year long, and keep them safe.

I've never met a teacher who makes the conscious decision "I'll teach badly this year in order to prepare my kids for more bad teaching." Every educator hopes to be remembered by students as someone who made a difference in their lives, whether it happens over the course of a year in one teacher's classroom or over a sustained experience in a great elementary school. But it's hard to buck the pressure of administrators, curriculum coordinators, even our colleagues, for full-scale adoption of test-driven programs. If all else fails, one way to persevere is to use a mandated program selectively, and then close the door and clear time and space for authentic work and the kinds of relationships with students that brought you into the profession in the first place.

Authentic relationships are rooted in authentic schoolwork. The work is the crucible—a child's initiative, questions, understandings, and misunderstandings, matched with a teacher's knowledge of children, methods, and the disciplines he or she teaches. No one bonds with kids over a program-in-a-box, a test-prep curriculum, or a standard.

For a small, rural school with a diverse student body, CTL has produced an astonishing number of high school valedictorians, prep schoolers on full scholarships, and Ivy League stars. But the true measure of the school's success is to be found in the sense and satisfaction that students and teachers derive from the culture that thrives here and the systems we develop here—small change upon small change that transform all our lives.

Works Cited

Atwell, Nancie. 1998. *In the Middle: New Understandings About Writing, Reading, and Learning.* Second Edition. Portsmouth, NH: Heinemann.

_____. 2002. *Lessons That Change Writers.* Portsmouth, NH: firsthand/Heinemann.

_____. 2006. *Naming the World: A Year of Poems and Lessons.* Portsmouth, NH: firsthand/Heinemann.

_____. 2007. *The Reading Zone: How to Help Kinds Become Skilled, Passionate, Habitual, Critical Readers.* New York: Scholastic.

_____. 2011. *Reading in the Middle: Workshop Essentials.* Portsmouth, NH: Heinemann.

_____. 2011. *Writing in the Middle: Workshop Essentials.* Portsmouth, NH: Heinemann.

Bazelon, Emily. 2013. *Sticks and Stones: Defeating the Culture of Bullying and Rediscovering the Power of Character and Empathy.* New York: Random House.

Burns, Marilyn. 2007. *About Teaching Mathematics: A K–8 Resource.* Sausalito, CA: Math Solutions Publications.

Clay, Marie. 1985. *The Early Detection of Reading Difficulties.* Third Edition. Portsmouth, NH: Heinemann.

Coffin, Helene. 2009. *Every Child a Reader: Month-by-Month Lessons to Teach Beginning Reading.* New York: Scholastic.

Davis, Stan. 2007. *Schools Where Everyone Belongs: Practical Strategies for Reducing Bullying.* Second Edition. Champaign, IL: Research Press.

DeMille, Ted. 2008. *Making Believe on Paper: Fiction Writing with Young Children.* Portsmouth, NH: Heinemann.

Fountas, Irene and Gay Su Pinnell. 1998. *Word Matters: Teaching Phonics and Spelling in the Reading/Writing Classroom.* Portsmouth, NH: Heinemann.

Gladwell, Malcolm. 2008. *Outliers: The Story of Success.* Boston: Little, Brown.

Graves, Donald. 2003. *Writing: Teachers and Children at Work.* 20th Anniversary Edition. Portsmouth, NH: Heinemann.

Hakim, Joy. 1993–2005. *A History of US, Volumes 1–10.* New York: Oxford University Press.

Harvey, Stephanie and Harvey Daniels. 2009. *Comprehension and Collaboration: Inquiry Circles in Action.* Portsmouth, NH: Heinemann.

Heard, Georgia. 2012. *A Place for Wonder: Reading and Writing Nonfiction in the Primary Grades.* Portland, ME: Stenhouse.

Horn, Martha and Mary Ellen Giacobbe. 2007. *Talking, Drawing, Writing: Lessons for Our Youngest Writers.* Portland, ME: Stenhouse.

Johnston, Peter. 2004. *Choice Words.* Portland, ME: Stenhouse.

Murray, Donald. 1993. *Write to Learn.* Fort Worth, TX: Holt, Rinehart, and Winston.

Murray, Miki. 2004. *Teaching Mathematics Vocabulary in Context: Windows, Doors, and Secret Passageways.* Portsmouth, NH: Heinemann.

Murray, Miki and Jennifer Jorgensen. 2007. *The Differentiated Math Classroom: A Guide for Teachers, K–8.* Portsmouth, NH: Heinemann.

Newkirk, Thomas. 2012. *The Art of Slow Reading.* Portsmouth, NH: Heinemann.

Newkirk, Thomas and Penny Kittle, Editors. 2013. *Children Want to Write: Donald Graves and the Revolution in Children's Writing.* Portsmouth, NH: Heinemann.

Nichols, Eugene D. and Sharon Schwartz. 1997. *The Mathematics Dictionary and Handbook.* Honesdale, PA: Nichols Schwartz Publishing.

O'Connell, Susan and John SanGiovanni. 2013. *Putting the Practices into Action.* Portsmouth, NH: Heinemann.

Paley, Vivian. 1992. *You Can't Say You Can't Play.* Cambridge: Harvard University Press.

Powers, Glenn. 2014 (forthcoming). *Reader's Roundtable: Conversations at the Core of a Reading Classroom.* Portland, ME: Stenhouse.

Reimer, Luetta and Wilbert Reimer. 1994. *Mathematicians Are People, Too: Stories from the Lives of Great Mathematicians.* Lebanon, IN: Seymour Publications.

Sibberson, Franki. 2003. *Still Learning to Read.* Portland, ME: Stenhouse.

Sibberson, Franki. 2008. *Day-to-Day Assessment in the Reading Workshop: Making Informed Instructional Decisions in Grades 3–6.* New York: Scholastic.

Szymusiak, Karen, Franki Sibberson, and Lisa Koch. 2008. *Beyond Leveled Books: Supporting Early and Transitional Readers in Grades K–5.* Portland, ME: Stenhouse.